Pocket Book

All you have to know !

ENGLISH - THAI

Pocket book, 6th print 2007

Text by

Georg Gensbichler

Sarika Puangsombat

ISBN 974-93618-0-6

Illustrations by

BanDon

Published by

Internet: www.bangkokbooks.com

E-mail: info@bangkokbooks.com

Fax Thailand: (66) - 2 - 517 1009

Copyright Bangkok Book House

Printed in Thailand

The publishers wish to thank **Mr. Sylvester van Welij** for all his effort and help in making this revised edition possible.

All rights reserved. No part of this book may be reproduced, copied, stored or transmitted in any form without prior written permission from the publisher.

ENGLISH - THAI

All you have to know !

Contents

THAI LANGUAGE 10
Polite syllables 12
The Thai alphabet 13

GREETINGS 18
First examples 20

VERBS 24
What you always hear 25
Additional verbs 28

ADJECTIVES 38

QUESTION & ANSWER 44
Questions words 45
YES and NO 49
Additional words 50

CONTENTS

NUMBERS & COUNTING 52
Counting 54
Classification 55

TIME & DATE 56
Time 57
Date 60
Months 61
Additional words 63
Examples: time 64
Do you have time ? 67

SHOPPING 70
Additional words 72
Toilet articles 73
Colours 74
Comparison 75

LIVING 78
House and apartment 79
Living room 80
Bathroom 80
Kitchen 81
Bedroom 82

CONTENTS

WORKING 84
Occupation --- Job 85
Business & School 87

FAMILY 88
Relatives 90

DOCTOR'S OFFICE 92
Body 95
Illness 97

POST OFFICE & BANK 100
Important words 101
Examples: Post Office & Bank ... 103

TELEPHONE 106

NATURE 110
Animals --- Plants 111

CONTENTS

TRAVEL *116*
Examples: Travelling *118*
Travelling by car *120*
Travelling by train *123*
City and Country *124*
Directions *125*
More examples *126*

FEELINGS *130*
'Heart' - words *131*
Additional words *136*

LOVE *138*
Get to know... .... *139*
Love stories *143*
Farewell *145*

IMPORTANT PHRASES *148*
What you will hear all the times ! *149*

Contents

- RESTAURANT & BAR 152
- Important words 154
- Drinks 155
- Fruits 157
- Cooking terms 158
- Taste & Flavour 159
- Spices 159
- Thai spices 160
- Small snacks 162
- Breakfast 163
- Salads 164
- Soups 165
- Curry 167
- Rice dishes 168
- Pasta 169
- Seafood 170
- Dishes - quick and easy 173
- Sweets 174
- At the restaurant 176
- In the bar 179

INDEX 182

OTHER BOOKS

Need to know more ?

The fun way to learn the language !

ENGLISH - THAI
The fun way to learn the language...

Includes colloquial Thai !

www.bangkokbooks.com

INTRODUCTION

THAI   LANGUAGE

Introduction

*This extended version of our popular **"English - Thai - Holidays Language - Guide"** covers a wider range of the Thai language and should be helpful for the tourist as also for the foreigner living in Thailand. One should be able to understand the most important phrases and have some small talk with the Thai people.*

The Romanized words in this book are only an approximation, as there are sounds in Thai which don't have an exact English equivalent. In addition it is important to learn the exact pronunciation from a Thai or you risk being misunderstood.

Correct pronunciation of the different tones:

The different tones:

Thai is a tonal language so it is also essential to learn the correct tone when you learn the word. There are 5 tones. Romanized words that look the same can therefore have up to 5 different meanings.

INTRODUCTION

Introduction to the 5 different tones:

1. middle tone:

without symbol   *common tone, pronounced flat
all syllables without symbol should
be pronounced flat in this book*

        e.g.: **maa** = *come*   มา

2. low tone:

symbol: ↓   *similar to middle tone
voice drops lower than normal*

        e.g.: **m↓ai** = *new*   ใหม่

3. falling tone:

symbol: ⌢   *pronounced falling
like an emphatic pronunciation in
English*

        e.g.: **m⌢ai** = *not*   ไม่

INTRODUCTION

4. high tone:

symbol: ◌́ usually the most difficult.
voice goes up higher than normal

e.g.: **máa** = **horse** ม้า

5. rising tone:

symbol: ◌̌ like the English question tone

e.g.: **mǎa** = **dog** หมา

Polite syllables

Whenever you speak Thai you should use the syllable **'khráp'** *or* **'khǎ'** *at the end of the sentence.*
If you are male you use **'khráp'** *and if you are female you use* **'khǎ'** *at the end of each sentence.*

INTRODUCTION

The Thai alphabet

Following a list of all consonants and vowels of the Thai alphabet.

consonant	initial	final	closest English	note
ป	p	p	spit	not aspirated
ต ฏ	t	t	step	not aspirated
ก	k	k	skin	not aspirated
พ ภ ผ	ph	p	pen	aspirated p, never as: phone
ท ฑ ฒ ธ ถ ฐ	th	t	tea	aspirated t, never as: the
ค ฆ ข	kh	k	king	aspirated k
บ	b	p	bed	
ด ฎ	d	t	dock	
จ	j	t	jet	
ม	m	m	man	
น ณ	n	n	nine	
ง	ng	ng	sing	can also occur at the beginning
ฟ ฝ	f	p	fit	
ส ศ ษ ซ	s	t	sit	
ห ฮ	h		hall	

13

INTRODUCTION

consonant	initial	final	closest English	note
ฉ ช ฌ	ch	t	check	
ร	r	n	room	
ล ฬ	l	n	lock	
ว	w	w	wing	
ย ญ	y	i	young	
อ	-	-	(silent)	used if begins with vowel sound

```
ก ข ฃ ค ฅ ฆ ง จ ฉ ช ซ ฌ ญ ฎ ฏ ฐ
ฑ ฒ ณ ด ต ถ ท ธ น บ ป ผ ฝ พ ฟ
ภ ม ย ร ล ว ศ ษ ส ห ฬ อ ฮ
```

```
-ะ -า -ิ -ี -ึ -ื -ุ -ู เ-ะ เ-
แ-ะ แ- โ-ะ โ- เ-าะ อ -ัวะ -ัว
เ-ียะ เ-ีย เ-ือะ เ-ือ เ-อะ เ-อ -ำ
ใ- ไ- เ-า ฤ ฤๅ ฦ ฦๅ
```

INTRODUCTION

The vowels can be positioned before, after, above or under the consonants.

long vowel	phonetic	English	Thai word	meaning
-า	aa	plaza	plaa	fish
เ-	e	plain	khet	zone
แ-	ae	pan	mae	mother
ี-	ee	green	mee	have
โ-	oh	home	lohk	world
-อ	aw	lawn	hawng	room
ู-	uu	moon	muu	pork
ื-อ ื-	ue	lure	mue	hand
เ-อ เ-ิ-	oe	fur	doen	walk
ไ- ใ-	ai	dye	mai	not
-าว	aao	brow	khaao	rice
ัว -ว-	ua	poor	wua	cow
เ-ือ	uea	pure	kluea	salt
เ-ีย	ia	beer	mia	wife
เ-ียว	io	new	khio	green
เ-ือย	uei		nuei	tired
เ-ย	oei		khoei	ever

15

INTRODUCTION

short vowel	phonetic		English	Thai word	meaning
-ะ	-ั-	a' a	far	rak	love
เ-ะ	เ-็-	e' e	let	lek	small
แ-ะ	แ-็-	ae' ae	mat	lae'	and
-ิ	-ิ-	i' i	feet	khit	think
โ-ะ	--	o' o	boat	phop	meet
เ-าะ		o'	lot	ko'	island
-ุ	-ุ-	u' u	book	thuk	every
-ึ	-ึ-	ue' ue	luck[1]	khuen	rise
เ-อะ		oe'	hut[2]	yoe'	many
ไ-		ai			
เ-า		ao	loud	bao	light
-ัวะ		ua'			
เ-ือะ		uea'			
เ-ียะ		ia'		pawpia'	spring roll
-ำ		am	farm	nam	water

Notes:

[1] like in French "tu" or German "Umlaut - u (ü)"

[2] not too far from the English hut (think of "Pizza hut"). Another example could be the golf term "putt", or the more familiar "nut"

Log on to **www.bangkokbooks.com** and see a full list of available titles.

Online ordering available - we deliver worldwide!

GREETINGS - FIRST WORDS

GREETINGS

GREETINGS - FIRST WORDS

Good Morning !		
Good Afternoon !	Sawatdee khrap (kha) !	
Good Evening !	สวัสดี ครับ (ค่ะ)	
I (male)	**phom**	**ผม**
I (female)	**dee chan, chan**	**ดิฉัน, ฉัน**
you	khun	คุณ
he, she	khao	เขา
it	man	มัน
we	(phuak)rao	พวกเรา
you	(phuak)khun	พวกคุณ
they	(phuak)khao	พวกเขา
mine, my	khawng phom	ของผม
mine, my	khawng chan	ของฉัน
yours	khawng khun	ของคุณ
his, her	khawng khao	ของเขา
our	khawng phuakrao	ของพวกเรา
yours	khawng phuakkhun	ของพวกคุณ
theirs	khawng phuakkhao	ของพวกเขา

GREETINGS - FIRST WORDS

First examples...

Welcome to Thailand

Yindee tawn rap !
ยินดีต้อนรับ

How are you ?

Sabaai dee mai khrap ?
สบายดีไหมครับ

Thanks, fine.

Sabaai dee khrap.
สบายดีครับ

What is your name ?

Khun chue arai khrap ?
คุณชื่ออะไรครับ

My name is...

Phom chue...
ผมชื่อ...

I am glad to meet you.

Phom dee jai tee dai phop khun.
ผมดีใจที่ได้พบคุณ

Thank you.

Khawp khun khrap.
ขอบคุณครับ

GREETINGS - FIRST WORDS

I don't understand.

Phǒm mâi khâo jai.
ผมไม่เข้าใจ

Please speak more slowly !

Chûai phûut cháa cháa nòi !
ช่วยพูดช้าๆหน่อย

Please speak louder !

Chûai phûut dang dang nòi !
ช่วยพูดดังๆหน่อย

Please say again !

Chûai phûut èek khráng !
ช่วยพูดอีกครั้ง

How do you call this in Thai ?

Nêe phaasǎa Thai rîak wâa arai ?
นี่ภาษาไทยเรียกว่าอะไร

GREETINGS - FIRST WORDS

Do I pronounce it correctly?

Phom awk siang thuuk mai khrap?
ผมออกเสียงถูกไหมครับ

Bye bye.

Laa gawn.
ลาก่อน

See you later.

Laeo phop kan na'.
แล้วพบกันนะ

See you tomorrow.

Phrung nee phop kan.
พรุ่งนี้พบกัน

See you soon.

Laeo phop kan mai.
แล้วพบกันใหม่

Good luck.

Chohk dee na'!
โชคดีนะ

My regards to...

Faak khwaam khit thueng...
ฝากความคิดถึง...

GREETINGS - FIRST WORDS

VERBS

VERBS

What you always hear...

ask	thǎam	ถาม
be	pen	เป็น
be (located)	yùu	อยู่
buy	súe	ซื้อ
can, be able	dâi	ได้
carry	thǔe *(things)*	ถือ
carry	ûm *(persons)*	อุ้ม
come	maa	มา
do, make	tham	ทำ
drink	dùem	ดื่ม
eat	kin (thaan) khâao	กินข้าว, ทานข้าว
find	phóp	พบ
forget	luem	ลืม
give	hâi	ให้
go	pai	ไป
go out	pai thîo	ไปเที่ยว
have	mee	มี
hear	dâi yin	ได้ยิน

25

VERBS

help	chûai	ช่วย
know	rúu jàk	รู้จัก
laugh	hǔa ró'	หัวเราะ
like	châwp	ชอบ
live, reside	yùu	อยู่
look	duu, mawng	ดู, มอง
look for, search	hǎa	หา
love	rák	รัก
must	tâwng	ต้อง
need, want	tâwng kaan	ต้องการ
pay	jàai ngoen	จ่ายเงิน
play	lên	เล่น
read	àan	อ่าน
remember	jam	จำ
see	hěn	เห็น
sell	khǎai	ขาย
sit	nâng	นั่ง
sleep	nawn	นอน
smile	yím	ยิ้ม

VERBS

speak	phûut	พูด
swim	wâai náam	ว่ายน้ำ
take	ao	เอา
tell	bàwk	บอก
understand	khâo jai	เข้าใจ
wait	raw	รอ
want	yàak	อยาก
wash, launder	sák	ซัก
wash, shampoo	sà	สระ
wash, clean	láang	ล้าง
work	tham ngaan	ทำงาน
write	khĭan	เขียน

sák phâa = *wash clothes* ซักผ้า
sà' phŏm = *shampoo one's hair* สระผม
láang mue = *wash one's hands* ล้างมือ

27

VERBS

Additional verbs

AAA

accompany	song	ส่ง
add up	buak	บวก
advertise	tham khohsanaa	ทำโฆษณา
agree	hen duai	เห็นด้วย
announce	pra'kaat	ประกาศ
answer	toop	ตอบ
arrive	maa thueng	มาถึง
assist, help	chuai luea	ช่วยเหลือ
assume	sommat	สมมติ
attack	johm tee	โจมตี

BBB

begin, start	roem	เริ่ม
believe	chuea	เชื่อ
bet	phanan	พนัน
blossom	baan	บาน
borrow	khaw yuem	ขอยืม
break	hak	หัก

VERBS

build	sâang	สร้าง

CCC

call (phone)	thoh pai hăa	โทรไปหา
cancel	yók lôek	ยกเลิก
celebrate	chalăwng	ฉลอง
change	plìan	เปลี่ยน
chase away	lâi, lâi pai	ไล่, ไล่ไป
check, examine	trùat	ตรวจ
climb	peen	ปีน
close	pìt	ปิด
collect	sà'sŏm	สะสม
command	sàng	สั่ง
complain	bòn	บ่น
convince	tham hâi chûea mân	ทำให้เชื่อมั่น
cook	tham kap khâao	ทำกับข้าว
correct	kâekhăi	แก้ไข
count	náp lêk	นับเลข
cry	ráwng hâi	ร้องให้
cut	tàt	ตัด

VERBS

DDD

dance	tenram	เต้นรำ
deliver	faak	ฝาก
deliver	song hai	ส่งให้
dig	kut	ขุด
discover	khon phop	ค้นพบ
divide	haan	หาร
dream	fan	ฝัน
dust	pat fun	ปัดฝุ่น

EEE

end, finish	loek	เลิก
escape, flee	nee	หนี
explain	athibaai	อธิบาย
export	song awk	ส่งออก

FFF

feed	hai aahaan	ให้อาหาร
feel	ruusuek	รู้สึก
find	phop	พบ

VERBS

flirt	láo lohm	เล้าโลม
follow	tit taam	ติดตาม
forecast, predict	tham naai	ทำนาย
fry	thâwt	ทอด

GGG

gain (weight)	phôem nám nàk	เพิ่มน้ำหนัก
gather, assemble	rûam kan	ร่วมกัน
get up	tùen	ตื่น
give	yók hâi	ยกให้
go down(stairs)	long bandai	ลงบันได
go for a walk	doen lên	เดินเล่น
go up(stairs)	khûen bandai	ขึ้นบันได
grow	plùuk	ปลูก

HHH

hang	khwǎen	แขวน
happen	kòet	เกิด
hate	klìat	เกลียด
hide	sâwn	ซ่อน
hit	tee	ตี

VERBS

hope	wǎng	หวัง
hunt	lâa	ล่า

I I I, JJJ

ice-skate	lên sakét	เล่นสเก็ต
import	nam khâo	นำเข้า
interrupt	khat jang wa'	ขัดจังหวะ
invent	pradit	ประดิษฐ์
invite	chuan	ชวน
joke	phûut talòk	พูดตลก
jump	kra'dòht	กระโดด

KKK

kick	tè'	เตะ
kiss	hǎwm	หอม
kiss (on the cheeks)	jùup	จูบ
knock (ring the bell)	kòt krading	กดกระดิ่ง
knock (on the door)	khó' pra'tuu	เคาะประตู

LLL

leave, abandon	àwk jàak	ออกจาก

32

VERBS

lend	hai yuem	ให้ยืม
let, lease, rent out	hai chao	ให้เช่า
lie	kohhok	โกหก
listen	fang	ฟัง
look after, take care	fao	เฝ้า
lose	phae	แพ้

MMM

manage	jat kaan	จัดการ
marry	taeng ngaan	แต่งงาน
misunderstand	khao jai phit	เข้าใจผิด
mow	tat yaa	ตัดหญ้า
multiply	khoon	คูณ

NNN

need, require	jaai	จ่าย

OOO

open	poet	เปิด
order	sang	สั่ง

VERBS

PPP

paint	thaa sĕe	ทาสี
pay	kèp ngoen	เก็บเงิน
persuade	chák chuan	ชักชวน
pick up, come for	ráp	รับ
pick up, lift	yók, kèp	ยก, เก็บ
plough, plow	thǎi naa	ไถนา
point to	chée	ชี้
pour	the	เท
prevent	pâwng kan	ป้องกัน
produce	phàlìt	ผลิต
pull	dueng	ดึง
punch	tòi	ต่อย
punish	long thôht	ลงโทษ
push	plàk	ผลัก

QQQ

quarrel	thá'ló'	ทะเลาะ

VERBS

RRR

receive	dai rap	ได้รับ
register	long thabian	ลงทะเบียน
remove, clear away	kep khong	เก็บของ
renew	taw aayu'	ต่ออายุ
rent, lease	chao	เช่า
repair	sawm	ซ่อม
respect	khaorop	เคารพ
rest	phak, phak nuei	พัก, พักเหนื่อย
run	wing	วิ่ง

SSS

send	song	ส่ง
shoot	ying	ยิง
shout	ta'kohn	ตะโกน
sing	rawng phleng	ร้องเพลง
slimming	lot nam nak	ลดน้ำหนัก
smell	domklin	ดมกลิ่น
smoke	suup buree	สูบบุหรี่
spell	sa'kot	สะกด

35

VERBS

stand	yuen	ยืน
start, begin	roem	เริ่ม
stitch, sew	yep	เย็บ
subtract	lop	ลบ
suggest	sanoe	เสนอ
suppose, guess	songsai	สงสัย

TTT

take a ride	khap rot len	ขับรถเล่น
taste	chim	ชิม
teach	sawn	สอน
think	khit	คิด
throw	paa, yohn	ปา, โยน
touch, grab	jap	จับ
translate	plae	แปล
travel	doenthaang	เดินทาง
try	phayaayaam	พยายาม
try, attempt	phayaayaam, lawng	พยายาม, ลอง

36

VERBS

VVV

vaccuum, hoover	dùut fùn	ดูดฝุ่น
visit	pai hǎa, yîamyian	ไปหา, เยี่ยมเยียน

WWW

wake up	plùk	ปลุก
walk	doen	เดิน
waste	sǐa	เสีย
whisper	krà'sîp	กระซิบ
win	chaná'	ชนะ
wipe	chêt	เช็ด
work on, deal with	triam	เตรียม

ADJECTIVES

ADJECTIVES

ADJECTIVES

big	yài	ใหญ่
small	lék	เล็ก
cheap	thùuk	ถูก
expensive	phaeng	แพง
clean	sà àat	สะอาด
dirty	sòkkàpròk	สกปรก
dangerous	antaraai	อันตราย
safe	plàwt phai	ปลอดภัย
dark	mûet	มืด
light	sàwàang	สว่าง
easy	ngâai	ง่าย
difficult	yâak	ยาก
empty	wâang, plào	ว่าง, เปล่า
full	tem	เต็ม
fat	uan	อ้วน
thin, slim	phawm	ผอม
thick	nǎa	หนา
thin	baang	บาง
good	dee	ดี
bad	leo	เลว

39

ADJECTIVES

hard	**khaeng**	**แข็ง**
soft	**num / awn**	**นุ่ม / อ่อน**
hot	rawn	ร้อน
cold	naao / yen	หนาว/เย็น
illegal	**phit kot maai**	**ผิดกฎหมาย**
legal	**thuuk kot maai**	**ถูกกฎหมาย**
light	bao	เบา
heavy	nak	หนัก
little	**noi**	**น้อย**
a lot, plenty	**maak**	**มาก**
loud	dang	ดัง
quiet	bao	เบา
near	**klai**	**ใกล้**
far	**klai**	**ไกล**
old	kao	เก่า
new	mai	ใหม่
old	**kae**	**แก่**
young (girl)	**saao**	**สาว**
young (boy)	**num**	**หนุ่ม**

Be careful with the pronunciation!

40

ADJECTIVES

ordinary	thammadaa	ธรรมดา
special	pheeset	พิเศษ
poor	**jon**	**จน**
rich	**ruai**	**รวย**
ripe	suk	สุก
unripe	dip	ดิบ
shallow	**tuen**	**ตื้น**
deep	**luek**	**ลึก**
short	san	สั้น
long	naan	นาน
short	**san**	**สั้น**
long	**yaao**	**ยาว**
silly	ngoh	โง่
clever	chalaad	ฉลาด
skilful	**keng**	**เก่ง**
clumsy	**ngum ngaam**	**งุ่มง่าม**
slow	chaa	ช้า
quick	reo	เร็ว
tidy, neat	**riap roi**	**เรียบร้อย**
untidy	**loe' thoe'**	**เลอะเทอะ**

41

ADJECTIVES

ugly	kheere	ขี้เหร่
beautiful	suai	สวย
weak	**awn ae**	**อ่อนแอ**
strong	**khaeng raeng**	**แข็งแรง**
wide	kwaang	กว้าง
narrow	khaep	แคบ
wet	**piak**	**เปียก**
try	**haeng**	**แห้ง**
wrong	phit	ผิด
right	thuuk	ถูก

New idea for a book ?

Are you looking for a publisher for your book ?

Talented writer ?

Would you like to publish a book ?

Contact us!

Bangkok Book House

Bangkok, Thailand

Fax: **(66) - 2 - 517 1009**

E-mail: *info@bangkokbooks.com*

Internet: *www.bangkokbooks.com*

QUESTION & ANSWER

QUESTION and ANSWER

QUESTION & ANSWER

Questions words

> There are two ways to form a question:
> **1.** use any of the listed question words
> *or*
> **2.** add the word **'mai'** at the end of the sentence

How ?	yang ngai	ยังไง
How far ?	klai thaorai	ไกลเท่าไร
How many ?	kee	กี่
How much ?	thaorai	เท่าไร
What ?	arai	อะไร
When ?	mue-arai	เมื่อไร
Why ?	thammai	ทำไม
Where ?	theenai	ที่ไหน
Where from ?	jaak nai	จากไหน
Where to ?	(pai) nai	(ไป) ไหน
Which ?	(an) nai	(อัน) ไหน
Which way ?	thaang nai	ทางไหน
Who ?	khrai	ใคร
Who ?	(khon) nai	(คน) ไหน

QUESTION & ANSWER

When will you come back again ?

Khun ja' klap maa <u>mue-arai</u> ?
คุณจะกลับมาเมื่อไร

Why don't you have a girlfriend ?

<u>Thammai</u> khun mai mee faen ?
ทำไมคุณไม่มีแฟน

What do you work ?

Khun tham ngaan <u>arai</u> ?
คุณทำงานอะไร

Who (which person) can speak Thai ?

<u>Khon nai</u> phuut phaasaa thai dai ?
คนไหนพูดภาษาไทยได้

Who can speak Thai ?

<u>Khrai</u> phuut phaasaa thai dai ?
ใครพูดภาษาไทยได้

QUESTION & ANSWER

Which sunglasses do you like ?

Khun châwp waêntaa <u>an năi</u> ?
คุณชอบแว่นตาอันไหน

How far is it to the market ?

Talàat <u>klai thâorai</u> jàak theênee ?
ตลาดไกลเท่าไรจากที่นี่

How do you do that ?

Nêe tham <u>yaang ngai</u> ?
นี่ทำยังไง

How much is it ?

Raakhaa <u>thâorai</u> ?
ราคาเท่าไร

How many siblings do you have ?

Khun mee peenáwng <u>kèe</u> khon ?
คุณมีพี่น้องกี่คน

QUESTION & ANSWER

Where do you live ?
Khun phák yuù theenǎi ?
คุณพักอยู่ที่ไหน

Where do you come from ?
Khun maa jàak nǎi ?
คุณมาจากไหน

Where do you go?
Khun pai nǎi ?
คุณไปไหน

Which is the way to the market ?
Thaang nǎi pai talàat ?
ทางไหนไปตลาด

> *To form a question without question word, just add the word **'mǎi'** to the end of the sentence.*

Can you speak Thai ?
Khun phûut phaasǎa thai dâi mǎi ?
คุณพูดภาษาไทยได้ไหม

QUESTION & ANSWER

YES and NO

1) *There is no easy answer for **YES** or **NO** in the Thai language.*
   All depends on the asked question.

   > Yes --- No
   > *Just repeat the verb of the question to say*
   > **YES**
   > *Add the particle **'mâi'** (=not) in front of the verb of the question to say*
   > **NO**

2) *Many times the question will end with the particle*
   '...châi mǎi' (= isn't it?)
   *The answer with **'châi'** means **YES** and*
   *'mâi châi' means **NO**.*

yes	châi	ใช่
no	mâi châi	ไม่ใช่

3) *You can also use the particle **'khráp'** or **'khâ'** for*
   YES
   *and **'mâi khráp'** or **'mâi khâ'** for **NO**.*

yes	khráp / khâ	ครับ / ค่ะ
no	mâi khráp / mâi khâ	ไม่ครับ / ไม่ค่ะ

QUESTION & ANSWER

Additional words

question	kham thaam	คำถาม
answer	kham tawp	คำตอบ
already	laeo	แล้ว
also, too	duai	ด้วย
although	yaang rai ko dee	อย่างไรก็ดี
and, and then	lae', laeo ko	และ, แล้วก็
because	phro' waa	เพราะว่า
but	tae	แต่
if, when	thaa	ถ้า
in case of	phuea waa	เผื่อว่า
maybe, perhaps	aat ja'	อาจจะ
nevertheless	mae waa	แม้ว่า
only	thaonan	เท่านั้น
or	rue	หรือ
or not yet?	laeo rue yang	แล้วหรือยัง
possibly	khong ja'	คงจะ
with	kap	กับ
yet, not yet	yang, yang mai	ยัง, ยังไม่

www.bangkokbooks.com

You are in a hurry ?

All you need to know to keep going.

This little book will help you get by in Thailand!

NUMBERS and COUNTING

NUMBERS & COUNTING

Numbers

๐	0	sǔun	ศูนย์
๑	1	nùeng	หนึ่ง
๒	2	sǎwng	สอง
๓	3	saam	สาม
๔	4	sèe	สี่
๕	5	hâa	ห้า
๖	6	hòk	หก
๗	7	jèt	เจ็ด
๘	8	pàet	แปด
๙	9	gâo	เก้า
๑๐	10	sìp	สิบ
๑๑	11	sìp-èt	สิบเอ็ด
๑๒	12	sìp-sǎwng	สิบสอง
๒๐	20	yêe-sìp	ยี่สิบ
๒๑	21	yêe-sìp-èt	ยี่สิบเอ็ด
๓๐	30	sǎam-sìp	สามสิบ
๑๐๐	100	nùeng rói	หนึ่งร้อย
๓๒๕	325	sǎam rói yêe-sìp-hâa	สามร้อยยี่สิบห้า

53

NUMBERS & COUNTING

๑๐๐๐	1.000	nueng phan	หนึ่งพัน
๑๐๐๐๐	10.000	nueng muen	หนึ่งหมื่น
๑๐๐๐๐๐	100.000	nueng saen	หนึ่งแสน
๑๐๐๐๐๐๐	1,000.000	nueng laan	หนึ่งล้าน

dozen	loh	โหล
pair	khuu	คู่
first time	khrang raek	ครั้งแรก
last time	khrang sut thaai	ครั้งสุดท้าย

Counting

2 children   luuk sawng khon   ลูกสองคน
(child - 2 - classification)

3 cars   rot saam khan   รถสามคัน
(car - 3 - classification)

> *If you can't remember the correct particle,*
> *you can use the word **'an'**.*

NUMBERS & COUNTING

Classification

To count things or people in the Thai language, you have to use special words, particles (classification). You just add this particle to the word.

There are about 80 different particles !

particle for	particle	
cars	khan	คัน
trees	ton	ต้น
flowers, joss sticks	dawk	ดอก
letters, newspapers	chabap	ฉบับ
books, candles, knives	lem	เล่ม
elect. appliances (TV, radio)	khrueang	เครื่อง
fruits	luuk	ลูก
houses, closet, cupboard	lang	หลัง
dress, suit	chut	ชุด
small things	**an**	อัน
people	khon	คน
glasses, dishes, photos	bai	ใบ
animals, clothes, furniture	tua	ตัว

55

TIME & DATE

TIME & DATE

Time

'tee': night time

0:00	thiang khuen	เที่ยงคืน
1:00	tee nueng	ตีหนึ่ง
2:00	tee sawng	ตีสอง
3:00	tee saam	ตีสาม
4:00	tee see	ตีสี่
5:00	tee haa	ตีห้า

'mohng chao': morning

6:00	hok mohng chao	หกโมงเช้า
7:00	nueng mohng chao	หนึ่งโมงเช้า
8:00	sawng mohng chao	สองโมงเช้า
9:00	saam mohng chao	สามโมงเช้า
10:00	see mohng chao	สี่โมงเช้า
11:00	haa mohng chao	ห้าโมงเช้า

57

TIME & DATE

'baai mohng': afternoon

12:00	thi-ang wan	เที่ยงวัน
13:00	baai (nueng) mohng	บ่าย(หนึ่ง)โมง
14:00	baai sawng mohng	บ่ายสองโมง
15:00	baai saam mohng	บ่ายสามโมง
16:00	baai see mohng	บ่ายสี่โมง
17:00	baai haa mohng	บ่ายห้าโมง

'thum': evening

18:00	hok mohng yen	หกโมงเย็น
19:00	nueng thum	หนึ่งทุ่ม
20:00	sawng thum	สองทุ่ม
21:00	saam thum	สามทุ่ม
22:00	see thum	สี่ทุ่ม
23:00	haa thum	ห้าทุ่ม

TIME & DATE

14:30	baai sawng mohng khrueng บ่ายสองโมงครึ่ง
14.50	eek sip naathee baai saam mohng อีกสิบนาทีบ่ายสามโมง

> *Be careful:*
> *9 o'clock in the morning (= **3 mohng chao**)*
> *3 o'clock in the afternoon (= **baai 3 mohng**)*
> *9 o'clock in the evening (= **3 thum**)*

What is the time?	Kee mohng laeo	กี่โมงแล้ว
time	welaa	เวลา
hour	chua mohng	ชั่วโมง
half hour	khrueng chua mohng	ครึ่งชั่วโมง
minute	naathee	นาที
second	winaathee	วินาที
watch, clock	naalikaa	นาฬิกา

TIME & DATE

Date

Monday	wan jan	วันจันทร์
Tuesday	wan angkhaan	วันอังคาร
Wednesday	wan phut	วันพุธ
Thursday	wan pharuehat	วันพฤหัส
Friday	wan suk	วันศุกร์
Saturday	wan sao	วันเสาร์
Sunday	wan aathit	วันอาทิตย์
today	wan nee	วันนี้
yesterday	muea waan nee	เมื่อวานนี้
tomorrow	phrung nee	พรุ่งนี้
after tomorrow	ma'ruen nee	มะรืนนี้
before yesterday	muea waan suen	เมื่อวานซืน
morning	tawn chao	ตอนเช้า
afternoon	tawn baai	ตอนบ่าย
evening	tawn yen	ตอนเย็น
day / night	wan / khuen	วัน / คืน

TIME & DATE

weekend	sao-aathit	เสาร์อาทิตย์
week	aathit	อาทิตย์

Months

January	makaraa khom	มกราคม
February	kumphaa phan	กุมภาพันธ์
March	meenaa khom	มีนาคม
April	mesaa yon	เมษายน
May	phruetsaphaa khom	พฤษภาคม
June	mithunaa yon	มิถุนายน
July	karakadaa khom	กรกฎาคม
August	singhaa khom	สิงหาคม
September	kanyaa yon	กันยายน
October	tulaa khom	ตุลาคม
November	phruetsajikaa yon	พฤศจิกายน
December	thanwaa khom	ธันวาคม
month	duean	เดือน
beginning of month	ton duean	ต้นเดือน
end of month	plaai duean	ปลายเดือน

TIME & DATE

> *There are 3 seasons in Thailand:*
> *1) **rueduu rawn**: March - June*
> *2) **rueduu fon**: July - October*
> *3) **rueduu naao**: November - February*

season	rueduu	ฤดู
hot season	rueduu rawn	ฤดูร้อน
rainy season	rueduu fon	ฤดูฝน
cool season	rueduu naao	ฤดูหนาว
year	pee	ปี
century	satawat	ศตวรรษ
date	wan tee	วันที่

> ***Date in Thai:***
> ***wan tee** + **number** + **month***
> *for example :   August 16th =*
> ***wan tee   16 (= sip hok)   singhaa kho***
> วันที่   ๑๖   สิงหาคม

TIME & DATE

Additional words

after, when	lang jaak	หลังจาก
always	samoe, talawt pai	เสมอ, ตลอดไป
appointment, date	mee nat	มีนัด
approximate	pra'maan	ประมาณ
at, on	tee	ที่
before, ago	tee laeo	ที่แล้ว
before, previous	gawn	ก่อน
be late	maa chaa, maa saai	มาช้า, มาสาย
constant, permanent	talawt welaa	ตลอดเวลา
ever	khoei	เคย
in, still	eek	อีก
in this moment	kamlang	กำลัง
in time	than welaa	ทันเวลา
just	phoeng, muea kee	เพิ่ง, เมื่อกี้
just now	dio nee, tawn nee	เดี๋ยวนี้, ตอนนี้
last	tee laeo	ที่แล้ว
meeting	nat phop	นัดพบ
nearly, almost	kueap ja'	เกือบจะ

TIME & DATE

next	naa	หน้า
normally	pokatee	ปกติ
on time	trong welaa	ตรงเวลา
since	tangtae	ตั้งแต่
sometimes	baang khrang	บางครั้ง
soon	reo reo nee	เร็วๆนี้
urgent	reep	รีบ
waste of time	sia welaa	เสียเวลา

Examples: time

Sorry for being late !

Khaw thoht tee maa chaa !
ขอโทษที่มาช้า

Sorry for let you waiting !

Khaw thoht tee tham hai khun raw !
ขอโทษที่ทำให้คุณรอ

TIME & DATE

Sorry for disturbing you !

Khǎw thôht têe róp kuan khun !
ขอโทษที่รบกวนคุณ

Sorry, but I am busy !

Khǎw thôht phǒm mee thura' !
ขอโทษผมมีธุระ

You should come here on time !

Khun khuan ja' maa theenee trong welaa !
คุณควรจะมาที่นี่ตรงเวลา

How long more ?

Mee welaa èek thǎorai ?
มีเวลาอีกเท่าไหร่

Time is up !   Time to go.

Mot welaa !   Dâai welaa laéo.
หมดเวลา   ได้เวลาแล้ว

65

TIME & DATE

I have to adjust my watch.

Phǒm tâng welaa.
ผมตั้งเวลา

My watch is 3 minutes fast.

Naalíkaa phǒm reo pai sǎam naathee.
นาฬิกาผมเร็วไปสามนาที

My watch is 3 minutes late.

Naalíkaa phǒm cháa pai sǎam naathee.
นาฬิกาผมช้าไปสามนาที

My watch goes exactly.

Naalíkaa phǒm trong welaa.
นาฬิกาผมตรงเวลา

My watch stopped working.

Naalíkaa taai.
นาฬิกาตาย

TIME & DATE

Do you have time?

Do you have time?

Waang mai? Mee welaa mai?
ว่างไหม, มีเวลาไหม

About when?

Tawn nai? Pra'maan kee mohng?
ตอนไหน, ประมาณกี่โมง

Is that too early?

Reo koen pai rue plao?
เร็วเกินไปหรือเปล่า

When is it okay?

Khun saduak mue-arai?
คุณสะดวกเมื่อไหร่

Whenever.

Mue-rai ko dai.
เมื่อไหร่ก็ได้

Always.

Talawt welaa.
ตลอดเวลา

TIME & DATE

You say when it's best.
Khun waang mue-arai bawk phom.
คุณว่างเมื่อไหร่บอกผม

I have no time.
Mai waang. Kamlang yung.
ไม่ว่างกำลังยุ่ง

That's a bad day for me.
Wan nan mai waang.
วันนั้นไม่ว่าง

This day is okay.
Wan nan ko dai.
วันนั้นก็ได้

Come later.
Dio maa.
เดี๋ยวมา

Come again.
Maa eek na'.
มาอีกนะ

TIME & DATE

SHOPPING

SHOPPING

> **'sài sûea'** = *put on (clothes)* — ใส่เสื้อ
> **'tòt sûea'** = *take off (clothes)* — ถอดเสื้อ
> **'tàeng tua'** = *dress nicely* — แต่งตัว

clothes	sûea phâa	เสื้อผ้า
belt	khěmkàt	เข็มขัด
blouse	sûea	เสื้อ
dress	chút	ชุด
gloves	thǔng mue	ถุงมือ
hat, cap	mùak	หมวก
jacket	sûea jacket	เสื้อแจ็กเก็ท
pyjamas	chút nawn	ชุดนอน
sandal	rawng tháo tae'	รองเท้าแตะ
shirt	sûea	เสื้อ
shoe	rawng tháo	รองเท้า
skirt	kra'prohng	กระโปรง
sock	thǔng tháo	ถุงเท้า

SHOPPING

suit	suut	สูท
sweater	suea naao	เสื้อหนาว
towel	phaa chet tua	ผ้าเช็ดตัว
trouser	kaang keng	กางเกง
T-shirt	suea yuet	เสื้อยืด

Additional words

bag	kra'pao	กระเป๋า
cotton	phaa faai	ผ้าฝ้าย
hand-made	tham duai mue	ทำด้วยมือ
leather	nang sat	หนังสัตว์
made from...	tham duai	ทำด้วย
market	talaat	ตลาด
present	khawng khwaan	ของขวัญ
quality	khunaphaap	คุณภาพ
sale	lot raakhaa	ลดราคา
silk	phaa mai	ผ้าไหม
special offer	lot phiset	ลดพิเศษ
tailor	raan tat suea	ร้านตัดเสื้อ
type, sort, kind	chanit	ชนิด

SHOPPING

Toilet articles

brush	praeng	แปรง
comb	wĕe	หวี
hair shampoo	yaa sà' phŏm	ยาสระผม
lipstick	lipsatik	ลิปสติก
make-up	khrŭeang săm aang	เครื่องสำอาง
nail scissors	kankrai tat lép	กรรไกรตัดเล็บ
perfume	nám hŏwm	น้ำหอม
powder	păeng	แป้ง
razor, shaver	mêet kohn	มีดโกน
shaving cream	kreem kohn nuat	ครีมโกนหนวด
soap	sabùu	สบู่
toothbrush	praeng sĕe fan	แปรงสีฟัน
toothpaste	yaa sĕe fan	ยาสีฟัน

'praeng fan' = *brush one's teeth* แปรงฟัน
'kohn nuat' = *shave* โกนหนวด

SHOPPING

Colours

colour	sĕe	สี
black	dam	ดำ
brown	námtaan	น้ำตาล
dark blue	nám ngoen	น้ำเงิน
dark brown	námtaan khêm	น้ำตาลเข้ม
dark green	khĭo kàe	เขียวแก่
gold	thawng	ทอง
grey	thăo	เทา
light blue	fáa	ฟ้า
light green	khĭo àwn	เขียวอ่อน
orange	sôm	ส้ม
pink	chomphuu	ชมพู
red	daeng	แดง
silver	ngoen	เงิน
violet	muang	ม่วง
white	khăao	ขาว
yellow	lŭeang	เหลือง

SHOPPING

Comparison

> 1st : adjective + **kwaa**
> 2nd : adjective + **thee sut**
>
> z.B.: **big -- bigger -- biggest**
> yai -- yai kwaa -- yai thee sut
> หญ่ ใหญ่กว่า ใหญ่ที่สุด

I am going shopping.

Phom/chan pai sue khong.
ผม/ฉันไปซื้อของ

How much is it ?

Raakhaa thaorai ?
ราคาเท่าไหร่

75

SHOPPING

That's a little bit too expensive !

Phaeng pai noi !
แพงไปหน่อย

That's too expensive !

Phaeng koen pai !
แพงเกินไป

Can you reduce the price ?

Lot (raakhaa) dai mai ?
ลด(ราคา)ได้ไหม

Do you have something cheaper ?

Thuuk kwaa nee mee mai ?
ถูกกว่านี้มีไหม

Do you have it in a different colour ?

Mee see uen eek mai ?
มีสีอื่นอีกไหม

SHOPPING

Can I try it on ?

Khǎw lawng sài dâi mǎi ?
ขอลองใส่ได้ไหม

That's too big - too small / too long - too short / too wide - too tight.

Nêe yài-lék / yaao-sân / luam-khap koen pai.
นี่ใหญ่-เล็ก / ยาว-สั้น / หลวม-คับ เกินไป

Do you have a bigger size ?

Khun mee thêe yài kwàa née mǎi khráp/khà ?
คุณมีที่ใหญ่กว่านี้ไหมครับ/ค่ะ

LIVING

LIVING

House and apartment

> **cháo baân** = rent a house   เช่าบ้าน
> **cháo hâwng** = rent a room   เช่าห้อง
> **khâa cháo** = the rent   ค่าเช่า

carpet	phrom	พรม
door	pra'tuu	ประตู
elevator, lift	lif	ลิฟ
entrance	thaang khâo	ทางเข้า
exit	thaang àwk	ทางออก
fence	rúua	รั้ว
floor	phúen	พื้น
garden	sǔan	สวน
house	bâan	บ้าน
library	hâwng sàmùt	ห้องสมุด
stairs, ladder	bandai	บันได
storey, floor	chán	ชั้น
swimming pool	sà' wâai nám	สระว่ายน้ำ
wall	phànǎng	ผนัง
window	nâa tàang	หน้าต่าง

LIVING

Living room

> **hâwng nâng lên** = *living room* ห้องนั่งเล่น

bookshelf	chán waang nǎngsǔe	ชั้นวางหนังสือ
chair	kâo-êe	เก้าอี้
radio	withayú'	วิทยุ
sofa	sofa	โซฟา
table	tó'	โต๊ะ
telephone	thohrasàp	โทรศัพท์
television	thohratát	โทรทัศน์

Bathroom

> **hâwng nám** = *bathroom* ห้องน้ำ

bathtub	àang àap nám	อ่างอาบน้ำ
mirror	krà'jòk	กระจก
toilet	chakrôhk	ชักโครก
washbasin	àang láang nâa	อ่างล้างหน้า
water tap	káwk nám	ก็อกน้ำ

Kitchen

hawng khrua = *kitchen* ห้องครัว

bottle opener	thee poet khuat	ที่เปิดขวด
cooking pot	maw	หม้อ
fridge	tuu yen	ตู้เย็น
frying pan	kra' tha'	กระทะ
garbage bin, dustbin	thang khaya'	ถังขยะ
kitchen cupboard	chan waang jaan	ชั้นวางจาน
microwave oven	microwave	ไมโครเวฟ
sink	aang laang jaan	อ่างล้างจาน
stove, oven	tao op	เตาอบ
stove (electric)	tao fai faa	เตาไฟฟ้า
stove (gas)	tao gas	เตาแก๊ส
thermos flask	kratik nam rawn	กระติกน้ำร้อน

Living

Bedroom

hǎwng nawn = *bedroom* ห้องนอน

bed	tiang nawn	เตียงนอน
blanket	phâa hòm	ผ้าห่ม
coat hanger	mái khwǎen sûea	ไม้แขวนเสื้อ
drawer	lín chák	ลิ้นชัก
lamp	khohm fai	โคมไฟ
make-up table	to' khrûeang paêng	โต๊ะเครื่องแป้ง
mattress	thêe nawn	ที่นอน
pillow	mǎwn	หมอน
wardrobe, closet	tûu sûea phâa	ตู้เสื้อผ้า

www.bangkokbooks.com

New idea for a book?

Are you looking for a publisher for your book?

Talented writer?

Would you like to publish a book?

Contact us!

Bangkok Book House

Bangkok, Thailand

Fax: ***(66) - 2 - 517 1009***

E-mail: ***info@bangkokbooks.com***

Internet: ***www.bangkokbooks.com***

WORKING

WORKING

Occupation --- Job

What work do you do?

Khun tham ngaan arai khrap?
คุณทำงานอะไรครับ

Where do you work?

Khun tham ngaan theenai khrap?
คุณทำงานที่ไหนครับ

What is your profession?

Khun mee aacheep arai khrap?
คุณมีอาชีพอะไรครับ

profession	aacheep	อาชีพ
hobby	ngaan adeerek	งานอดิเรก
employee	phanak ngaan	พนักงาน
worker	khon ngaan	คนงาน

WORKING

cook (man)	phaw khrua	พ่อครัว
cook (woman)	mae khrua	แม่ครัว
dentist	maw fan	หมอฟัน
doctor	maw, phaet	หมอ, แพทย์
electrician	chaang fai faa	ช่างไฟฟ้า
engineer	witsawakon	วิศวกร
farmer	chaao naa	ชาวนา
fisherman	chaao pra'mong	ชาวประมง
hairdresser	chaang tham phom	ช่างทำผม
lawyer	thanaai kwaam	ทนายความ
maid	khon rap chai	คนรับใช้
mechanic	chaang kon	ช่างกล
musician	nak dontree	นักดนตรี
nurse	phayaabaan	พยาบาล
painter	chaang thaa see	ช่างทาสี
photographer	chaang phaap	ช่างภาพ
pilot	nak bin	นักบิน
policeman	tamruat	ตำรวจ
postman	bu rut praisanee	บุรุษไปรษณีย์

WORKING

secretary	le khaa nu kaan	เลขานุการ
soldier	thahaan	ทหาร
teacher	khruu, aajaan	ครู, อาจารย์
tailor	chaang tat suea	ช่างตัดเสื้อ

Business & School

businessman	nak thurakit	นักธุรกิจ
company	borisat	บริษัท
factory	rohng ngaan	โรงงาน
manager	phuu jat kaan	ผู้จัดการ
owner	jao khawng	เจ้าของ
shop	raan	ร้าน
school	rohng rian	โรงเรียน
primary school	prathom sueksaa	ประถมศึกษา
secondary school	mathayom sueksaa	มัธยมศึกษา
college, academy	withayaalai	วิทยาลัย
university	mahaawithayaalai	มหาวิทยาลัย
student, pupil	nak rian	นักเรียน
test, exam	sawp	สอบ

FAMILY

FAMILY

Family

family	khrawp khrua	ครอบครัว
parents	phaw mae	พ่อ, แม่
father	phaw	พ่อ
mother	mae	แม่
wife	phanrayaa	ภรรยา
husband	saamee	สามี
son	luuk chaai	ลูกชาย
daughter	luuk saao	ลูกสาว
grandchild	laan	หลาน
younger brother	**nawng** chaai	น้องชาย
elder brother	**phee** chaai	พี่ชาย
younger sister	nawng saao	น้องสาว
elder sister	phee saao	พี่สาว
siblings	phee nawng	พี่, น้อง

You have to distinguish between younger and elder persons.
'nawng' *(younger person)* น้อง
'phee' *(elder person)* พี่

FAMILY

Relatives

> *You have to distinguish between relatives from your father's and mother's sides of the family.*

relatives	yaat	ญาติ
grandfather (of father)	paw	ปู่
grandfather (of mother)	taa	ตา
grandmother (of father)	yaa	ย่า
grandmother (of mother)	yaai	ยาย
uncle (=brother from father)	aa, lung	อา, ลุง
uncle (=brother from mother)	naa, lung	น้า, ลุง
aunt (=sister from father)	aa, paa	อา, ป้า
aunt (=sister from mother)	naa, paa	น้า, ป้า
niece	laan saao	หลานสาว
nephew	laan chaai	หลานชาย
father-in-law	phaw taa	พ่อตา
mother-in-law	mae yaai	แม่ยาย
son-in-law	luuk khoei	ลูกเขย
daughter-in-law	luuk sa'phai	ลูกสะใภ้

Small talk with bar girls...

Essential phrases and short conversations for the bar scene and more...

DOCTOR's OFFICE

DOCTOR'S OFFICE

maw = doctor	หมอ
maw fan = dentist	หมอฟัน
phayaabaan = nurse	พยาบาล
rawng phayaabaan = hospital	โรงพยาบาล

You should see a doctor.
Khit waa khun khuan pai haa maw.
คิดว่าคุณควรไปหาหมอ

I don't feel very well.
Ruusuek mai sabaai. Phom mai sabaai.
รู้สึกไม่สบาย, ผมไม่สบาย

I am feeling (getting) sick.
Ruusuek yaak aajian.
รู้สึกอยากอาเจียน

I feel dizzy.
Ruusuek wian hua.
รู้สึกเวียนหัว

DOCTOR'S OFFICE

I feel very weak (faintness).
Ruusuek ja' pen lom.
รู้สึกจะเป็นลม

Where does it hurt ?
Jep thee nai ?
เจ็บที่ไหน

It hurts here.
Jep trong nee.
เจ็บตรงนี้

Take three pills (twice) daily.
Kin yaa saam met wan la' khrang (sawng khrang).
กินยาสามเม็ดวันละครั้ง(สองครั้ง)

Help ! = chuai duai ! ช่วยด้วย

DOCTOR'S OFFICE

Body

body	raang kaai, tua	ร่างกาย, ตัว
ankle	khaw thao	ข้อเท้า
arm	khaen	แขน
back	lang	หลัง
beard	khrao	เครา
blood	lueat	เลือด
bone	kra'duuk	กระดูก
bottom, buttocks	kon	ก้น
brain	samawng	สมอง
breast	nom	นม
cheek	kaem	แก้ม
chest, breast	naaok	หน้าอก
chin	khaang	คาง
ear	huu	หู
elbow	khaw sawgh	ข้อศอก
eye	taa	ตา
eyebrow	khiw	คิ้ว
face	naa	หน้า

DOCTOR'S OFFICE

finger	níw	นิ้ว
fingernail	lép mue	เล็บมือ
foot	thaó	เท้า
forehead	nâa phàak	หน้าผาก
genitals	awaíyawá' phêt	อวัยวะเพศ
hair	phŏm	ผม
hand	mue	มือ
head	hŭa	หัว
heart	hŭa chai	หัวใจ
hip	sà' phôhk	สะโพก
knee	hŭa khào	หัวเข่า
leg	khăa	ขา
lip	rim fĕe pàak	ริมฝีปาก
liver	tàp	ตับ
lung	pàwt	ปอด
mouth	pàak	ปาก
muscle	klâam, klâam núea	กล้าม, กล้ามเนื้อ
mustache	nùat	หนวด
neck	lam khaw	ลำคอ
nerve	sên prà'sàat	เส้นประสาท

96

DOCTOR'S OFFICE

nose	jamuuk	จมูก
shoulder	baa, lai, baa lai	บ่า, ไหล่, บ่าไหล่
skin	phiw, phiw nang	ผิว, ผิวหนัง
sole	faa thao	ฝ่าเท้า
stomach	thawng	ท้อง
sweat	nguea	เหงื่อ
toenail	lep thao	เล็บเท้า
tongue	lin	ลิ้น
tooth	fan	ฟัน
waist	eo	เอว
wrist	khaw mue	ข้อมือ

Illness

disease, illness	pen rohk	เป็นโรค
burn	mee phlae mai	มีแผลไหม้
cold	pen wat	เป็นหวัด
cough	ai	ไอ
diarrhoea	thawng sia	ท้องเสีย

97

DOCTOR'S OFFICE

faint, unconscious	pen lom	เป็นลม
fever	mee khai	มีไข้
flu, influenza	khai wat yai	ไข้หวัดใหญ่
fracture	hak	หัก
hurt	jep, puat	เจ็บ, ปวด
ill, sick	puai, mai sabaai	ป่วย, ไม่สบาย
infection	tit chuea	ติดเชื้อ
insect bite	dohn malaeng kat	โดนแมลงกัด
injury	baat jep	บาดเจ็บ
pain	puat	ปวด
sore throat	jep khaw	เจ็บคอ
sprain	khlet	เคล็ด
sunburn	taet phao	แดดเผา
vomit	aajian	อาเจียน
wound	baat phlae	บาดแผล

DOCTOR'S OFFICE

Medical Treatment

aspirin	aesphairin	แอสไพริน
bandage	phaa phan phlae	ผ้าพันแผล
diet	lot aahaan	ลดอาหาร
examine	truat	ตรวจ
exercise	awk gam lang kaai	ออกกำลังกาย
health	sukhaphaap	สุขภาพ
injection	cheet yaa	ฉีดยา
medical treatment	raksaa, duu lae	รักษา, ดูแล
medicine	yaa	ยา
painkiller	yaa kae puat	ยาแก้ปวด
pill, tablet	yaa met	ยาเม็ด
plaster	phalastoe	พลาสเตอร์
prescription	bai sang yaa	ใบสั่งยา
sleeping pill	yaa nawn lap	ยานอนหลับ

POST OFFICE & BANK

POST OFFICE & BANK

Important words

account	banchee	บัญชี
airmail	praisanee aakaat	ไปรษณีย์อากาศ
bank	thanaakhaan	ธนาคาร
cheque	chek	เช็ค
envelope	sawng jotmaai	ซองจดหมาย
express	duan	ด่วน
interest	dawk bia	ดอกเบี้ย
letter	jotmaai	จดหมาย
letterbox, mailbox	tuu praisanee	ตู้ไปรษณีย์
money	ngoen	เงิน
parcel, box	haw, haw khawng	ห่อ, ห่อของ
stamp	sataem	แสตมป์
post card	praisanee yabat	ไปรษณียบัตร
post office	praisanee	ไปรษณีย์
receipt	bai set	ใบเสร็จ
telegram	thohralek	โทรเลข
traveller's cheque	chek doenthaang	เช็คเดินทาง

POST OFFICE & BANK

receive a letter	rap jotmaai	รับจดหมาย
register a letter	long tha'bian	ลงทะเบียน
send a letter	song jotmaai	ส่งจดหมาย
type a letter	phim jotmaai	พิมพ์จดหมาย
borrow money	khaw yuem ngoen	ขอยืมเงิน
change money	laek ngoen	แลกเงิน
deposit money	faak ngoen	ฝากเงิน
earn money	haa ngoen	หาเงิน
lend money	hai yuem ngoen	ให้ยืมเงิน
save money	kep ngoen	เก็บเงิน
spend money	chai ngoen, sia ngoen	ใช้เงิน, เสียเงิน
waste money	sia daai ngoen	เสียดายเงิน
withdraw money	thawn ngoen	ถอนเงิน
be in debt	pen nee	เป็นหนี้
economical	pra'yat ngoen	ประหยัดเงิน

POST OFFICE & BANK

Examples : Post Office & Bank

Where is the nearest post office ?

Praisanee thee klai theesut yuu theenai khrap/kha' ?

What time is the bank open ?

Thanaakaan poet kee mawng khrap/kha ?
ธนาคารเปิดกี่โมงครับ/ค่ะ

Can I change traveller's cheques here?

Khuen chek doenthaang thee nee dai mai ?
ขึ้นเช็คเดินทางที่นี่ได้ไหม

Can I see your passport ?

Khaw duu nangsue doenthaang noi dai mai ?
ขอดูหนังสือเดินทางหน่อยได้ไหม

POST & BANK

Can you give me some small change?

Laek ngoen noi dai mai ?
แลกเงินหน่อยได้ไหม

Please change to ....

Khaw laek ngoen pen ngoen.....
ขอแลกเงินเป็นเงิน....

How long does mail take to Europe?

Song jotmaai pai europe chai welaa thaorai ?
ส่งจดหมายไปยุโรปใช้เวลาเท่าไหร่

How much is a letter to Europe?

Song jotmaai pai europe raakhaa thaorai ?
ส่งจดหมายไปยุโรปราคาเท่าไหร่

www.bangkokbooks.com

Need to know more ?

The fun way to learn the language !

E_{NGLISH} - T_{HAI}

The fun way to learn the language...

Includes colloquial Thai !

www.bangkokbooks.com

TELEPHONE

TELEPHONE

TELEPHONE

> **thoh** = to phone — โทร
> **thoh pai** = phone somebody — โทรไป
> **thoh maa** = phone from somewhere — โทรมา
> **thoh klap** = phone back — โทรกลับ
> **toh saai** = connect — ต่อสาย

mobile phone, handy	thohrasap mue tue	โทรศัพท์มือถือ
telephone	thohrasap	โทรศัพท์
telephone bill	khaa thohrasap	ค่าโทรศัพท์
telephone book	samut thohrasap	สมุดโทรศัพท์
telephone box	tuu thohrasap	ตู้โทรศัพท์
telephone number	boe thohrasap	เบอร์โทรศัพท์
answer the phone	rap thohrasap	รับโทรศัพท์
phone somebody	thohrasap, thoh	โทรศัพท์, โทร

overseas call	thohrasap taang pra'thet โทรศัพท์ต่างประเทศ
collect call	thohrasap kep ngoen plaai thaang โทรศัพท์เก็บเงินปลายทาง
operator	panak ngaan rap thohrasap พนักงานรับโทรศัพท์

TELEPHONE

Who is speaking ?

Khrai phûut khráp ?
ใครพูดครับ

I dialled a wrong number.

Phǒm thoh phìt.
ผมโทรผิด

The line is busy.

Sǎai mâi wâang.
สายไม่ว่าง

There's no answer.

Mâi mee khrai ráp sǎai.
ไม่มีใครรับสาย

That will be all.

Khae nee na' khráp/kha'.
แค่นี้นะครับ/ค่ะ

One moment, please.

Raw sák khrûu khráp/kha. Khoi dǐo khráp/kha'.
รอสักครู่ครับ/ค่ะ คอยเดี๋ยวครับ/ค่ะ

TELEPHONE

Can I make an overseas call from here ?

Ja' thohrasap pai taang pra'thet jaak theenee dai mai ?

จะโทรศัพท์ไปต่างประเทศจากที่นี่ได้ไหม

Do you have a telephone listing ?

Mee samut thohrasap mai ?

มีสมุดโทรศัพท์ไหม

With whom would you like to speak ?

Tawng kaan phuut kap khrai khrap ?

ต้องการพูดกับใครครับ

Would you like to leave a message ?

Mee arai ja' sang mai ?

มีอะไรจะสั่งไหม

Please leave following message:

Karu'naa faak khaw khwaam duai na khrap/kha':

กรุณาฝากข้อความด้วยนะครับ/ค่ะ

NATURE

NATURE

Animals --- Plants

animal	sàt	สัตว์
flower	dàwk mái	ดอกไม้
grass	yăa	หญ้า
orchid	klûai mái	กล้วยไม้
palm tree	ton paam	ต้นปาล์ม
tree	ton mái	ต้นไม้
zoo	sŭan sàt	สวนสัตว์
ant	môt	มด
bird	nok	นก
butterfly	phĕe sĕua	ผีเสื้อ
cat	maeo	แมว
chicken	kài	ไก่
cockroach	malaeng sàap	แมลงสาบ
cow	wua	วัว
crocodile	jôra'khe	จระเข้
dog	măa	หมา
duck	pèt	เป็ด

111

Nature

elephant	chaang	ช้าง
fish	plaa	ปลา
fly	malaeng wan	แมลงวัน
frog	kop	กบ
horse	maa	ม้า
kangaroo	jingjoh	จิงโจ้
lion	sing toh	สิงโต
lizard	jing jok	จิ้งจก
monkey	ling	ลิง
mosquito	yung	ยุง
mouse, rat	nuu	หนู
parrot	nok gaeo	นกแก้ว
pig	muu	หมู
rabbit	kra'taai	กระต่าย
snake	nguu	งู
spider	maeng mum	แมงมุม
tiger	suea	เสือ
turtle	tao	เต่า

NATURE

> *'lom'* = wind ลม
> *'lom awn awn'* = breeze ลมอ่อนๆ
> *'lom chooi'* = breeze ลมโชย
> *'lom phat'* = windy ลมพัด
> *'lom phat raeng'* = very windy ลมพัดแรง

air	aakaat	อากาศ
bay	aao	อ่าว
beach	chaai haat	ชายหาด
cape	laem	แหลม
channel, canal	khlawng	คลอง
cloud	mek	เมฆ
coast	chaai tha'le	ชายทะเล
field	rai naa	ไร่นา
fire	fai	ไฟ
island	ko'	เกาะ
jungle	paa thuep	ป่าทึบ
lake	tha'le saap	ทะเลสาป
moon	pra' jan	พระจันทร์
mountain	phuukhao	ภูเขา

NATURE

river	mae nam	แม่น้ำ
sand	saai	ทราย
sea	tha'le	ทะเล
sky	faa	ฟ้า
star	daao	ดาว
stone	hin	หิน
sun	phra' aathit	พระอาทิตย์
sunrise	phra' aathit khuen	พระอาทิตย์ขึ้น
sunset	phra' aathit tok	พระอาทิตย์ตก
waterfall	nam tok	น้ำตก
weather	aakaat	อากาศ
wood, forest	paa	ป่า

> **'nam long'** = *low tide*   น้ำลง
> **'nam khuen'** = *high tide*   น้ำขึ้น
> **'nam thuam'** = *flood*   น้ำท่วม

www.bangkokbooks.com

New idea for a book ?

Are you looking for a publisher for your book ?

Talented writer ?

Would you like to publish a book ?

Contact us!

Bangkok Book House

Bangkok, Thailand

Fax: ***(66) - 2 - 517 1009***

E-mail: ***info@bangkokbooks.com***

Internet: ***www.bangkokbooks.com***

TRAVEL

TRAVEL

aircondition	khrueang aer	เครื่องแอร์
airplane	khrueang bin	เครื่องบิน
airport	sanaam bin	สนามบิน
arrival	thueng	ถึง
bicycle	rot jakrayaan	รถจักรยาน
bus (regular)	rot thammadaa	รถธรรมดา
bus (with aircondition)	rot prap aakaat	รถปรับอากาศ
bus station	sathaanee rot bas	สถานีรถบัส
bus stop	paai rot me	ป้ายรถเมล์
car	rot	รถ
crash helmet	muak kun nawk	หมวกกันน็อค
departure	awk	ออก
document	ekasaan	เอกสาร
ferry	ruea khaam faak	เรือข้ามฝาก
hotel	rong raem	โรงแรม
motorbike	rot jakrayaan yon	รถจักรยานยนต์
railway	rot fai	รถไฟ
railway station	sathaanee rot fai	สถานีรถไฟ
seaport, harbour	thaa ruea	ท่าเรือ
ship	ruea	เรือ

TRAVEL

> **hǎwng kûu** = *room with twin beds*   ห้องคู่
> **hǎwng dìo** = *room with double bed*   ห้องเดี่ยว

Examples: Travelling

Do you have rooms vacant?

Mee hǎwng wâang mǎi?
มีห้องว่างไหม

How much is it per night?

Khâa hǎwng wan la' thâorai?
ค่าห้องวันละเท่าไหร่

How long are you staying for?

Khun ja' yuu naan thâorai?
คุณจะอยู่นานเท่าไหร่

TRAVEL

I don't know yet how long.
Mai saap waa ja' yuu naan thaorai.
ไม่ทราบว่าจะอยู่นานเท่าไหร่

Can I see the room ?
Khaw duu hawng kawn dai mai ?
ขอดูห้องก่อนได้ไหม

Could you bring my luggage please?
Chuai yok kra'pao maa hai noi dai mai ?
ช่วยยกกระเป๋ามาให้หน่อยได้ไหม

Can I put something into the safe ?
Khaw faak khong wai nai tuu sef dai mai ?
ขอฝากของไว้ในตู้เซฟได้ไหม

Can I order food to the room ?
Sang aahaan maa thaan bon hawng dai mai ?
สั่งอาหารมาทานบนห้องได้ไหม

TRAVEL

My room number is...

Phom yuu hawng boe ...
ผมอยู่ห้องเบอร์...

I will depart tomorrow.

Phom ja' pai phrung nee.
ผมจะไปพรุ่งนี้

Travelling by car

> **tem tang** = *fill up* — เต็มถัง
> **khrueng tang** = *half full* — ครึ่งถัง

accident	ubati het	อุบัติเหตุ
break down	sia	เสีย
car	rot	รถ
car park	thee jawt rot	ที่จอดรถ
car rental charge	khaa chao rot	ค่าเช่ารถ
detour	thaang awm	ทางอ้อม
drive	wing	วิ่ง
drive, steer	khap	ขับ

TRAVEL

driving licence	bai khap khee	ใบขับขี่
garage	rhong kep rot	โรงเก็บรถ
insurance	pra'kan	ประกัน
intersection, junction	see yaek	สี่แยก
park	jawt rot	จอดรถ
petrol station	pam nam man	ปั๊มน้ำมัน
refuel	toem nam man	เติมน้ำมัน
short cut	thaang lat	ทางลัด
stop	jawt rot	จอดรถ
take a ride	nang rot len	นั่งรถเล่น
take over	saeng	แซง
tow off	laak rot	ลากรถ
traffic	ja raa jon	จราจร
traffic jam	rot tit	รถติด
traffic lights	fai ja raa jon	ไฟจราจร
turn	liao	เลี้ยว
turn around	klap rot	กลับรถ

TRAVEL

Please check the tyre pressure !

Chek lom yaang hai duai !
เช็คลมยางให้ด้วย

Can you repair the car here ?

Theenee sawm rot dai mai ?
ที่นี่ซ่อมรถได้ไหม

How long will it take to repair the car ?

Chai welaa sawm naan pra'maan thaorai ?
ใช้เวลาซ่อมนานประมาณเท่าไหร่

Where can I park the car ?

Jawt dai theenai ?
จอดได้ที่ไหน

I would like to rent a car.

Phom tawnkaan chao rot.
ผมต้องการเช่ารถ

Travelling by train

express train	rót duan	รถด่วน
fast train	rót reo	รถเร็ว
first class	chán nueng	ชั้นหนึ่ง
left-luggage office	thêe faak kra'pao	ที่ฝากกระเป๋า
platform	chaan cha laa	ชานชลา
railway	rót fai	รถไฟ
railway station	sathǎanee rót fai	สถานีรถไฟ
reservation	jawng tǔa	จองตั๋ว
return ticket	tǔa pai klap	ตั๋วไปกลับ
sleeping car	rót nawn	รถนอน
ticket	tǔa	ตั๋ว
ticket office	chawng khǎai tǔa	ช่องขายตั๋ว
timetable	taa raang rót fai	ตารางรถไฟ

Train to Chiang Mai leaves at 15:00 from platform 1.

Rót fai pai Chiang Mai ja awk chaan cha laa thêe 1 welaa baai 3 mohng.
รถไฟไปเชียงใหม่จะออกชานชลาที่ ๑ เวลาบ่าย ๓ โมง

TRAVEL

City and Country

> ***thit nuea*** = *north*   ทิศเหนือ
> ***thit tai*** = *south*   ทิศใต้
> ***thit ta'wan tok*** = *west*   ทิศตะวันตก
> ***thit ta'wan awk*** = *east*   ทิศตะวันออก

abroad	taang pra'thet	ต่างประเทศ
address	thee yuu	ที่อยู่
capital city	mueang luang	เมืองหลวง
city, town	mueang	เมือง
country	pra'thet	ประเทศ
district	amphoe	อำเภอ
lane	soi	ซอย
precinct	tambon	ตำบล
province	jangwat	จังหวัด
street	thanon	ถนน
village	muu baan	หมู่บ้าน
world	lohk	โลก
Europe	yurohp	ยุโรป
Thailand	thai	ไทย

TRAVEL

Australia	awsatrelia	ออสเตรเลีย
England	angkrit	อังกฤษ
USA	saharat amerika	สหรัฐอเมริกา
Cambodia	khamaen	เขมร
Laos	laao	ลาว
Malaysia	maalesia	มาเลเซีย
Myanmar	phamaa	พม่า

Directions

saai = left — ซ้าย
khwaa = right — ขวา
trong pai = straight ahead — ตรงไป

above	khaang bon	ข้างบน
around	rawp	รอบ
around the world	rawp lohk	รอบโลก
behind	daan lang	ด้านหลัง
corner	mum	มุม
here	thee nee	ที่นี่
in front	daan naa	ด้านหน้า

TRAVEL

in the middle of	trong klaang	ตรงกลาง
in, at	nai	ใน
inside	khaang nai	ข้างใน
next to, beside	daan khaang	ด้านข้าง
opposite	trong khaam	ตรงข้าม
outside	khaang nawk	ข้างนอก
over there	thee nohn	ที่โน่น
there	thee nan	ที่นั่น
under	khaang laang	ข้างล่าง
up to, as far as	jon thueng	จนถึง

More examples

Is this the way to Pattaya ?

Nee thanon pai Phathayaa chai mai ?
นี่ถนนไปพัทยาใช่ไหม

Which way to Pattaya ?

Pai Phathayaa pai thaang nai ?
ไปพัทยาไปทางไหน

TRAVEL

How long does it take to Pattaya ?

Pai Phathayaa chai welaa naan thaorai ?
ไปพัทยาใช้เวลานานเท่าไหร่

What time does the first (last) bus leave for Chonburi ?

Rot thio raek (sut thaai) pai Chonburee kee mohng ?
รถเที่ยวแรก(สุดท้าย)ไปชลบุรีกี่โมง

What a traffic jam today !

Wan nee rot tit maak chai mai ?
วันนี้รถติดมากใช่ไหม

Is it always like this ?

Pen yang nee thuk wan rue plao ?
เป็นยังงี้ทุกวันหรือเปล่า

You can bet on it.
There is always traffic like this.

Nae nawn. Rot tit yang nee thuk wan.
แน่นอน. รถติดอย่างนี้ทุกวัน

TRAVEL

I better walk.

Phǒm khít wâa phǒm dooen dee kwàa.
ผมคิดว่าผมเดินดีกว่า

It is too far to walk.

Thaang klai mâak.
ทางไกลมาก

Pleasant journey !

Thîo hâi sànùk ná' khráp !
เที่ยวให้สนุกนะครับ

Small talk with bar girls...

Essential phrases and short conversations for the bar scene and more...

FEELINGS

FEELINGS

'Heart' - words

> Many words which describe feelings begin or end with the word **'jai'**, which actually means **heart**.
>
> Following some important '**heart**' words with short explanations.

dee jai ดีใจ **glad**
*You can come back to Thailand after a long time and you will be feeling **'dee jai'**. This is used frequently for different occassions, but do not confuse it with **'jai dee'**.*

jai dam ใจดำ **careless, ruthless**
*Your friend needs your help, but you do not care.
They will say you are **'jai dam'**.*

jai dee ใจดี **nice, pleasant**
*You help somebody or you are doing somebody a favour without asking.
You will hear the compliment **'jai dee'**.*

FEELINGS

jai yen ใจเย็น **calm, cool**
You are in a traffic jam on your way to the airport and miss your plane. However, you are not angry, you stay cool, have 'jai yen'.
You will hear this word very often. Should you lose your temper, you will hear 'jai yen yen'.

jai ngâai ใจง่าย **easily influenced**
You are a person who can be easily manipulated, you do what others say.
You have an easy heart, have 'jai ngâai'.

jai nói ใจน้อย **sensitive**
Your heart is hurt easily. You are emotionally hurt very often.

jai pâm ใจป้ำ **generous**
You are going out with friends. When it's time to pay the bill, you pay everything. You are 'jai pâm'.

jai ráwn ใจร้อน **angry, upset**
You get upset easily. You have a 'hot heart', you are 'jai ráwn'. You will hear 'jai yen yen'.

FEELINGS

jep jai เจ็บใจ **hurt (emotionally)**
Your wife finds out that you have a minor wife. Your wife will feel 'jep jai'. Be careful.

jing jai จริงใจ **honest**
You are honest to others and say the truth. You don't hide your feelings
You have an 'honest heart', you are 'jing jai'.

chuen jai ชื่นใจ **pleased**
You are happy, pleased about something or somebody. You are 'chuen jai'.

klum jai กลุ้มใจ **concerned, worried**
Your daughter neglects her education and only enjoys her free time. You feel 'klum jai'.

hua jai หัวใจ **heart**
This means heart.

khao jai เข้าใจ **understand**
You understand what is said or done.

FEELINGS

kreng jai เกรงใจ **considerate, kind**
You are sitting in a non-smoking taxi. You do not care about this and smoke. The taxi driver does not say anything and lets you smoke.
He is 'kreng jai'.
This is one of the most important heart words.
Everybody will try to be 'kreng jai'.

mân jai มั่นใจ **confident**
You are absolutely sure about your feelings for your girlfriend. You are 'mân jai'. You also will hear this in TV spots and advertisements.

nâe jai แน่ใจ **sure**
You are sure about something, similar to 'mân jai'.

phuum jai ภูมิใจ **proud**
You are proud of something or somebody.
You are 'phuum jai'.

plaeg jai แปลกใจ **surprised**
If something surprises you, then you are 'plaeg jai' or also 'pralaat jai'.

FEELINGS

prathâp jai   ประทับใจ   **impressed**
Thailand impresses you.
*You are **'prathâp jai'** with Thailand.*

sǎbaai jai   สบายใจ   **happy**
You will hear this all the time.
It means happiness and satisfaction.

saô jai   เศร้าใจ   **heartbroken, sad**
This means broken heart. You feel sad, have no more
*interest in anything; you feel **'saô jai'**.*

sǐa jai   เสียใจ   **regret, sorrow, sad**
*If you feel sorry for a person, you say **'sǐa jai'**.*

sǒn jai   สนใจ   **interested**
You are interested in something or somebody.
*You feel **'sǒn jai'**.*

tâng jai   ตั้งใจ   **concentrate**
You are concentrating on what you are doing.
You put all your energy in a project.
*You are **'tâng jai'**.*

FEELINGS

Additional words

> ***aarom*** = mood — อารมณ์
> ***aarom dee*** = be in great mood — อารมณ์ดี
> ***aarom sia*** = be in bad mood — อารมณ์เสีย
> ***aarom ngut ngit*** = moody — อารมณ์หงุดหงิด

English	Thai (romanized)	Thai
afraid	klua	กลัว
ambitious, diligent	khayan	ขยัน
angry, furious	kroht, mohhoh	โกรธ, โมโห
annoyed	ramkhaan	รำคาญ
bored	buea	เบื่อ
brave, courageous	klaa haan	กล้าหาญ
cheerful	yindee	ยินดี
confused	sapson	สับสน
cowardly	mai klaa	ไม่กล้า
crazy	baa	บ้า
curious	yaak ruu yaak hen	อยากรู้อยากเห็น
disappointed	phit wang	ผิดหวัง
distrustful	song sai	สงสัย

FEELINGS

envious	it chaa	อิจฉา
excited	tuen ten	ตื่นเต้น
false	khee kohng	ขี้โกง
frustrated	kra'won krawaai	กระวนกระวาย
happy	mee khwaam suk	มีความสุข
jealous	hueng	หึง
lazy	khee kiat	ขี้เกียจ
lonely	ngao	เหงา
lovesickness	awk hak	อกหัก
miss	khit thueng	คิดถึง
nervous	ngut ngit	หงุดหงิด
pity	songsaan	สงสาร
playful	khee len	ขี้เล่น
shy	khee aai	ขี้อาย
stingy, mean	khee nio	ขี้เหนียว
worried	kang won	กังวล

rak = love   รัก
tok lum rak = fall in love   ตกหลุมรัก
rak saam sao = love triangle   รักสามเศร้า

137

LOVE

LOVE

Get to know...

Are you here alone ?

Khun maa khon dio rue plao ?
คุณมาคนเดียวหรือเปล่า

Do you like something to drink ?

Khun tawng kaan duem arai mai ?
คุณต้องการดื่มอะไรไหม

May I sit here ?

Nang duai dai mai ?
นั่งด้วยได้ไหม

Somebody sits here already ?

Theenee mee khon nang mai ?
ที่นี่มีคนนั่งไหม

What's your name ?

Khun chue arai ?
คุณชื่ออะไร

LOVE

Where do you live ?

Baân khun yùu theênai ?
บ้านคุณอยู่ที่ไหน

Where do you come from ?

Khun maa jàak nǎi ?
คุณมาจากไหน

How old are you ?

Khun aayu' thâorai ?
คุณอายุเท่าไหร่

What do you work ?

Khun tham ngaan àrai ?
คุณทำงานอะไร

Where do you work?

Khun tham ngaan theênai?
คุณทำงานที่ไหน

What do you do in your free time ?

Khun tham àrai welaa wâang ?
คุณทำอะไรเวลาว่าง

Do you come here often ?

Khun maa theênêe bòi mǎi ?
คุณมาที่นี่บ่อยไหม

LOVE

Should we go already ?

Pai kan rŭe yang ?
ไปกันหรือยัง

Let's go !

Pai kan daî laéo !
ไปกันได้แล้ว

I want to stay here longer.

Yàak yùu tàw èek nòi.
อยากอยู่ต่ออีกหน่อย

I will bring you home.

Phŏm ja' sòng khun klap baân.
ผมจะส่งคุณกลับบ้าน

I want to know more about you.

Phŏm yàak rúu jàk khun mâak kwàa née.
ผมอยากรู้จักคุณมากกว่านี้

LOVE

We think the same, don't we?

Rao khit muean kan chai mai?

เราคิดเหมือนกันใช่ไหม

Should we meet again?

Rao ja' phop kan eek mai?

เราจะพบกันอีกไหม

When can I meet you again?

Ja' phop khun eek muearai?

จะพบคุณอีกเมื่อไหร่

Can I have your telephone number?

Khaw boe thohrasap khun dai mai?

ขอเบอร์โทรศัพท์คุณได้ไหม

Can I call you?

Phom thoh haa khun dai mai?

ผมโทรหาคุณได้ไหม

LOVE

See you soon.
Rao phop kan eek.
แล้วพบกันอีก

See you tomorrow.
Phop kan phrung nee.
พบกันพรุ่งนี้

Take care.
Duulae tua eng duai na'.
ดูแลตัวเองด้วยนะ

Love stories

Love makes blind.
Kwaam rak tham hai khon taa bawt.
ความรักทำให้คนตาบอด

I am crazy for you.
Phom/Chan khlang khlai nai tua khun.
ผม/ ฉันคลั่งใคล้ในตัวคุณ

I love you.
Phom/Chan rak khun.
ผม/ฉันรักคุณ

LOVE

You are beautiful.
Khun suai jang loei.
คุณสวยจังเลย

You are handsome.
Khun law jang loei.
คุณหล่อจังเลย

You are so cute.
Khun naa rak jang loei.
คุณน่ารักจังเลย

*The words **jang loei** will be added here often, but actually don't have a meaning.*

You have beautiful eyes.
Taa khun suai jang loei.
ตาคุณสวยจังเลย

You have a wonderful smile.
Khun yim suai jang loei.
คุณยิ้มสวยจังเลย

LOVE

I want to stay with you.
Phŏm/Chán yàak yùu kàp khun.
ผม/ฉันอยากอยู่กับคุณ

Farewell

Will you send a letter?
Khun jà' khĭan jòtmǎai thŭeng chán rue plào.
คุณจะเขียนจดหมายถึงผม/ ฉันหรือเปล่า

I will send you a letter.
Phŏm jà' khĭan jòtmǎai thŭeng khun.
ผม/ ฉันจะเขียนจดหมายถึงคุณ

I will call you from England.
Phŏm jà' thoh hǎa khun jàak angkrit.
ผม/ฉันจะโทรหาคุณจากอังกฤษ

LOVE

I will come back soon.
Phom ja' klap maa reo reo nee.
ผมจะกลับมาเร็วๆนี้

I have to leave because of my job.
Phom tawng klap pai tham ngaan.
ผมต้องกลับไปทำงาน

Wait until I come back.
Raw phom klap maa na'.
รอผมกลับมานะ

Don't forget to write !
Yaa luem khian jotmaai maa baang na' !
อย่าลืมเขียนจดหมายมาบ้างนะ

Don't cry.
Yaa rong hai.
อย่าร้องไห้

Wipe your tears.
Chet nam taa.
เช็ดน้ำตา

LOVE

I can't take it.
Phom/Chan thon mai dai.
ผม/ฉันทนไม่ได้

I miss you.
Khit thueng khun.
คิดถึงคุณ

I have to think about you all the times.
Phom/Chan khit thueng khun samoe samoe.
ผม/ฉันคิดถึงคุณเสมอๆ

I will always love you.
Ja' rak khun talawt pai.
จะรักคุณตลอดไป

IMPORTANT PHRASES

Important PHRASES

IMPORTANT PHRASES

What you will hear all the times !

1. mâi pen rai ไม่เป็นไร **It doesn't matter !**
You will hear this phrase many times. You are in a traffic jam and miss your plane. You are desperate and upset. But you should relax and tell yourself 'mâi pen rai'.
Don't think Thais don't care. Don't misunderstand this phrase. Everybody just tries to cope with their fate and tries to stay calm whatever happens. There is no point in getting upset. The plane won't return..

2. jai yen yen ใจเย็นเย็น **calm, cool**
This phrase is widely used together with 'mâi pen rai'. It means 'cool heart'.
Stay calm and don't get upset or lose your temper. If you get angry, you will hear 'jai yen yen'.

3. sanuk สนุก **fun**
Thais love to have fun. They know how to entertain and have a good time.
Thais don't like to sit home alone. They enjoy going out together and having fun.
Even during a financial crisis everybody takes it easy and enjoys life as much as possible.

IMPORTANT PHRASES

We are sure you will have lots of fun in Thailand and won't get bored.

4. sabaai   สบาย   **happy**
*You will get asked '**sabaai mǎi?**' many times. '**Sabaai**' means happy and satisfied and '**mǎi**' is the particle to form a question. You will most probable answer '**sabaai mâak**'.*

5. double words
*Sometimes you will hear some words repeated. This is done to emphasis. Words, which are widely used, are for example '**mâak-maak**' (very much), '**jing - jing**' (100% sure), '**reo – reo**' (very fast), '**chaa – chaa**' (very slow) or also '**jai yen yen**' (cool heart).*

6. nicknames
*Most Thai people use nicknames instead of their real names. You will be surprised about some translations of these nicknames. These nicknames have meanings like '**rat**', '**pig**', '**sugar**' or even '**Pepsi**' like our Thai editor. But don't forget to use the particle '**Khun**' (= Mr., Mrs., Miss) with these nicknames.*
If your nickname is 'Fatty', don't get angry.

IMPORTANT PHRASES

7. rue plao, laeo rue yang   หรือเปล่า, แล้วหรือยัง
*Some questions end with **'rue plao'** or with **'laeo rue yang'**. This has the meaning of 'or not ?' and 'already or not yet?'.*

8. chai mai   ใช่ไหม
*Other questions end with **'chai mai'**. This can be translated with 'is it, isn't it'. (see also chapter question & answer, pages 44-51)*

9. dai mai   ได้ไหม
*Many questions end with **'dai mai'**. **'dai'** means 'to be able, can' and **'mai'** is the particle to form a question.*

10. riap roi   เรียบร้อย   **ready, okay**
*The question **'riap roi laeo ?'** means **Is everything ready, okay ?**.*

151

RESTAURANT & BAR

RESTAURANT and BAR

RESTAURANT & BAR

raan aahaan = smaller restaurant   ร้านอาหาร
phataakaan = bigger restaurant   ภัตตาคาร

aahaan = food   อาหาร
aahaan chao = breakfast   อาหารเช้า
aahaan klang wan = lunch   อาหารกลางวัน
aahaan yen = dinner   อาหารเย็น
aahaan kham = late night snack   อาหารค่ำ

hiw nam = thirsty   หิวน้ำ
hiw khaao = hungry   หิวข้าว

RESTAURANT & BAR

Important words

ashtray	thee khia bu'ree	ที่เขี่ยบุหรี่
bottle	khuat	ขวด
bottle opener	thee poet khuat	ที่เปิดขวด
bowl	chaam	ชาม
chair	kaoee	เก้าอี้
chopsticks	ta'kiap	ตะเกียบ
cigarettes	bu'ree	บุหรี่
cup	thuay	ถ้วย
drink	duem	ดื่ม
eat	kin khaao	กินข้าว
food	aahaan	อาหาร
fork	sawm	ซ้อม
glass	kaeo	แก้ว
knife	meet	มีด
lighter	fai chaek	ไฟแช็ค
market	talaat	ตลาด
matches	mai kheet fai	ไม้ขีดไฟ
menu	menuu	เมนู

RESTAURANT & BAR

napkin	kradaat	กระดาษ
plate	jaan	จาน
smoking	suup bu'ree	สูบบุหรี่
spoon	chawn	ช้อน
service, waiter	dek soef aahaan	เด็กเสริฟอาหาร
table	to'	โต๊ะ
tablecloth	phaa puu to'	ผ้าปูโต๊ะ
toothpick	mai jim fan	ไม้จิ้มฟัน

Drinks

water	nam	น้ำ
ice cubes	nam khaeng	น้ำแข็ง
coffee (hot or cold)	kaafae	กาแฟ
coffee (hot, milk & sugar)	kaafae rawn	กาแฟร้อน
iced coffee (milk & sugar)	kaafae yen	กาแฟเย็น
milk	nom	นม

---

mai sai nam taan = without sugar   ไม่ใส่น้ำตาล
ao waan waan = sweet   เอาหวานๆ
ao nom maak maak = with a lot of milk   เอานมมากๆ

155

RESTAURANT & BAR

tea (hot or cold)	chaa	ชา
tea (hot, milk & sugar)	chaa ráwn	ชาร้อน
iced tea (milk & sugar)	chaa yen	ชาเย็น
fruit juices	nám phǒnlamái	น้ำผลไม้

nám + name of fruit = fruit juice
for example: ***nám sàppàrót*** *= pineapple juice*

In Thailand one adds a little bit of salt to fresh fruit juices. If you would like to have your fruit juice without any salt, you say:
mâi sài kluea.

ไม่ใส่เกลือ

RESTAURANT & BAR

Fruits

phonlamai = *fruits*   ผลไม้

apple	aeppaen	แอปเปิ้ล
banana	kluai	กล้วย
coconut	ma'praao	มะพร้าว
durian	turian	ทุเรียน
grape	angun	องุ่น
guava	farang	ฝรั่ง
jackfruit	khanun	ขนุน
lime	ma'naao	มะนาว
longan	lamyai	ลำใย
lychee	linchee	ลิ้นจี่
mango	ma'muang	มะม่วง
mangosteen	mangkhut	มังคุด
orange	som	ส้ม
papaya	ma'la'kaw	มะละกอ
pineapple	sapparot	สับปะรด
pomelo	som-oh	ส้มโอ

RESTAURANT & BAR

rambutan	ngo'	เงาะ
roseapple	chomphuu	ชมพู่
sugarapple	noi naa	น้อยหน่า
tamarind	ma'khaam	มะขาม
watermelon	taeng moh	แตงโม

Cooking terms

***tham kap khaao* = cook**   ทำกับข้าว

bake	awp	อบ
boil	tom	ต้ม
chopped	sap	สับ
deep fry	thawt	ทอด
fry	phat	ผัด
grill	yaang, phao	ย่าง, เผา
raw	dip	ดิบ
stew, steam	nueng	นึ่ง
toast	ping	ปิ้ง
(well) done	suk	สุก

Restaurant & Bar

Taste & Flavour

> **rot** = *flavour* — รส
> **chim** = *to taste* — ชิม

bitter	khŏm	ขม
crisp	kràwp	กรอบ
salty	khem	เค็ม
sour	prîo	เปรี้ยว
spicy, hot	phèt	เผ็ด
sweet	wǎan	หวาน
sweet & sour	prîo - wǎan	เปรี้ยว - หวาน
tasteless	jèut	จืด

Spices

fish sauce	nám plaa	น้ำปลา
pepper	phrík thai	พริกไท
salt	kluea	เกลือ
sauce	sáws	ซอส
sugar	nám taan	น้ำตาล
vinegar	nám sôm sǎai chuu	น้ำส้มสายชู

RESTAURANT & BAR

Thai spices

nam jim   น้ำจิ้ม

sauce -- on nearly every table in all restaurants

nam som phrik dawng   น้ำส้มพริกดอง

vinegar-- with chilli

nam plaa   น้ำปลา

fisch sauce -- is used instead of salt

ka'pi'   กะปิ

shrimp paste-- made from very tiny shrimps

nam phrik ka'pi'   น้ำพริกกะปิ

shrimp sauce -- spicy

saws phrik   ซอสพริก

chilli sauce -- similar to ketchup, but spicy, with tomatos, garlic and chilli

RESTAURANT & BAR

nam phrik num — น้ำพริกหนุ่ม

chilli sauce -- from Northern Thailand, spicy, green colour

prik phao — พริกเผา

chilli -- chopped and roasted chillies

nam phrik phao — น้ำพริกเผา

chilli paste -- from *phrik phao*, garlic, onions and *nam plaa*

phrik pon — พริกป่น

chilli powder

seeiw khaao / seeiw dam — ซีอิ๊วขาว / ซีอิ๊วดำ

soy sauce -- called black or white soy sauce, but both are black in colour

nam man hoi — น้ำมันหอย

oyster sauce -- is used for cooking

RESTAURANT & BAR

Small snacks

> **kap klaem** = snack กับแกล้ม

shrimp chips	khaao kriap kung	ข้าวเกรียบกุ้ง
potato chips	man farang thawt	มันฝรั่งทอด
cashew nuts	met ma'muang thawt	เม็ดมะม่วงทอด
peanuts	thua thawt	ถั่วทอด
fish cake	thawt man plaa	ทอดมันปลา
roasted eggs	khai ping	ไข่ปิ้ง
meat balls	luuk chin ping	ลูกชิ้นปิ้ง
hot dog	sai krawk	ไส้กรอก
spring roll	paw pia' thawt	ปอเปี๊ยะทอด
satay	sa'te'	สะเต๊ะ
spare ribs	see khrohng muu thawt	ซี่โครงหมูทอด

> **som tam** = papaya salad --
> made from green papaya, lemon,
> sugar, fish sauce, tomato, garlic, tiny
> tried shrimps or crab and lots of
> chillies.
> Very spicy !

RESTAURANT & BAR

Breakfast

egg	khài	ไข่
boiled eggs	khài tôm	ไข่ต้ม
half boiled eggs	khài lûak	ไข่ลวก
plain omelet	khài jio	ไข่เจียว
stuffed omelet	khài yát sâi	ไข่ยัดไส้
scrambled eggs	khài khôn	ไข่คน
fried eggs	khài daao	ไข่ดาว
bread	khànŏm pang	ขนมปัง
butter	noei	เนย
jam, marmalade	yaem	แยม
honey	nám phûeng	น้ำผึ้ง

RESTAURANT & BAR

Salads

> **yam** = *Thai salad -- delicious, but very spicy. Is eaten as first course or small snack in the bar.*

prawn salad	yam kung	ยำกุ้ง
mixed salad	yam ruam mit	ยำรวมมิตร
glass noodle salad	yam wunsen	ยำวุ้นเส้น
seafood salad	yam ruam mit tha'le	ยำรวมมิตรทะเล
beef salad	yam nuea	ยำเนื้อ
squid salad	yam plaa muek	ยำปลาหมึก
sausage salad	yam sai krawk	ยำไส้กรอก

> **laap** = *Thai salad -- cooked and chopped, spicy, from Isaan (North-East Thailand)*

duck salad	laap pet	ลาบเป็ด
chicken salad	laap kai	ลาบไก่
beef salad	laap nuea	ลาบเนื้อ
pork salad	laap muu	ลาบหมู

RESTAURANT & BAR

Soups

> **khaao tom** = rice soup -- eaten for breakfast, with different ingredients available.   ข้าวต้ม
>
> **johk** = rice porridge -- similar to 'kaao tom', but thicker.   โจ๊ก

> **kuaitio nam** = noodle soup   ก๋วยเตี๋ยวน้ำ
>
> Following types of noodles are available:
>
> **sen yai** = thick noodles   เส้นใหญ่
>
> **sen lek** = thin noodles   เส้นเล็ก
>
> **sen mee** = very thin noodles   เส้นหมี่
>
> **ba' mee** = egg noodles   บะหมี่
>
> **kio** = wonton

RESTAURANT & BAR

> *tom yam* = *spicy - sour - soup*
> *probably the Thai national dish*

tom yam kung ต้มยำกุ้ง

prawn soup -- spicy, with lemon grass

tom yam po' taek, po' taek ต้มยำโป๊ะแตก, โป๊ะแตก

seafood soup -- with mussels, prawns, crabs, fish, etc.

Other soups

tom khaa kai ต้มข่าไก่

chicken soup --similar to *'tom yam'*, with coconut milk

tom juet wunsen muu sap ต้มจืดวุ้นเส้นหมูสับ

vegetable soup -- with chopped & minced pork (= muu sap) and glass noodles

tom som plaa ต้มส้มปลา

fish soup -- sour & spicy

Curry

kaeng ka'ree kai แกงกะหรี่ไก่

curry -- with coconut milk and chicken

kaeng khio waan muu แกงเขียวหวานหมู

curry -- green, sweet-sour curry with pork

kaeng phanaeng nuea แกงแพนงเนื้อ

curry -- thick curry with coconut milk and beef

kaeng phet kai แกงเผ็ดไก่

curry -- spicy, with red chillies and chicken

haw mok tha'le ห่อหมกทะเล

seafood curry -- thick, with coconut milk, steamed in banana leaves

Restaurant & Bar

Rice dishes

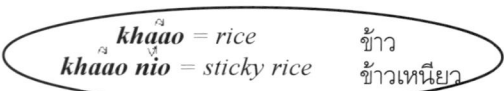

Rice is the main constituent in Thai food and there is an enormous varity of dishes with rice. Most dishes are served with rice and topped with chicken, pork, etc. Following a few typical dishes:

khaao man kai ข้าวมันไก่

chicken on rice -- thin cut chicken meat on rice with chicken soup

khaao muu daeng ข้าวหมูแดง

pork on rice -- red pork meat on rice

khaao muu krawp ข้าวหมูกรอบ

rice and pork -- crispy pork and rice

RESTAURANT & BAR

Pasta

kuaitio haeng   ก๋วยเตี๋ยวแห้ง

noodles without soup (see SOUPS, page 165 for different ingredients)

phat thai   ผัดไทย

fried noodles -- *'sen lek'* fried with prawns, vegetable, eggs and peanuts

phat seeiw   ผัดซีอิ๊ว

noodles with soy sauce -- *'sen yai'* fried with black soy sauce

khanom jeen nam yaa   ขนมจีนน้ำยา

noodles with fish curry

mee krawp   หมี่กรอบ

crisp noodles -- crispy fried noodles with prawns and bean sprouts

raat naa   ราดหน้า

noodles with thick sauce

Restaurant & Bar

Seafood

aahǎan thá'le = seafood อาหารทะเล

fish	plaa	ปลา
perch	plaa ka'phong	ปลากะพง
shark	plaa chalǎam	ปลาฉลาม
tuna	plaa oh	ปลาโอ
squid	plaa mùek	ปลาหมึก
oyster	hǒi naang rom	หอยนางรม
cockle	hǒi kraeng	หอยแครง
mussels	hǒi malaeng phùu	หอยแมลงภู่
clams	hǒi laai	หอยลาย
river crab	kang	กั้ง
crab	pûu	ปู
prawn	kûng	กุ้ง
lobster	kûng mang kon	กุ้งมังกร
tiger prawn	kûng kam kaam	กุ้งก้ามกาม

Restaurant & Bar

Seafood dishes

plaa prio waan ปลาเปรี้ยวหวาน

fish -- sweet & sour, with tomatos, pineapple, etc.

plaa thawt ปลาทอด

fish -- fried fish, dipping sauce

plaa nueng ma'naao ปลานึ่งมะนาว

fish -- steamed in lime sauce and chillies

plaa nueng pae' sa' ปลานึ่งแป๊ะซะ

fish -- steamed with mushrooms and coriander

plaa raat phrik ปลาราดพริก

fish -- fried with chilli dressing

plaa muek yat sai ปลาหมึกยัดไส้

squid -- filled with minced pork meat

hoi laai phat nam phrik phao หอยลายผัดน้ำพริกเผา

clams -- fried in chilli sauce

Restaurant & Bar

hǒi naang rom sòt   หอยนางรมสด

oyster -- on ice, with lime and onions

hǒi malaeng phûu àwp mâw din   หอยแมลงภู่อบหม้อดิน

mussels -- steamed, chilli sauce for dipping

kûng phǎo   กุ้งเผา

prawns -- grilled, chilli sauce for dipping

kûng chup páeng thâwt   กุ้งชุบแป้งทอด

prawns -- fried

kûng chae nam plaa   กุ้งแช่น้ำปลา

shrimps -- raw, with garlic, lime and chilli sauce

kûng mang kon phàt nâm phrík phǎo

lobster -- fried with chilli sauce   กุ้งมังกรผัดน้ำพริกเผา

kâam puu nûeng   ก้ามปูนึ่ง

crab -- steamed, chilli sauce for dipping

RESTAURANT & BAR

Dishes - quick and easy

khaao phat ข้าวผัด

fried rice -- with pork, chicken, crab or prawns available

kai phat nawmai ไก่ผัดหน่อไม้

chicken -- fried with bamboo sprouts

nuea phat nam man hoi เนื้อผัดน้ำมันหอย

beef -- fried in oyster sauce

muu phat kra'thiam prik thai หมูผัดกระเทียมพริกไทย

pork -- fried with garlic and pepper

kung phat nam phrik phao กุ้งผัดน้ำพริกเผา

prawns -- fried in roasted chillies

phat phak ruam mit ผัดผักรวมมิตร

vegetable -- fried for a short time only

Restaurant & Bar

Sweets

(*khanŏm* = sweets   ขนม)

nám khǎeng sǎi   น้ำแข็งใส

sweets -- sugar peas, beans, potatos, sticky rice, fruits, coconut creme, crushed ice

sǎng khayǎa   สังขยา

pudding -- made from pumpkin, eggs, sugar and coconut creme

fǒi tawng   ฝอยทอง

egg yolk -- fried in sweet syrup

khâao nǐo ma'muang   ข้าวเหนียวมะม่วง

sticky rice -- served with fresh mangos and coconut creme

khâao lǎam   ข้าวหลาม

sticky rice -- with coconut creme and black beans in the bamboo stick

RESTAURANT & BAR

khaao tom mat ข้าวต้มมัด

sticky rice -- in palm leaves with bananas and black beans

kluai chueam กล้วยเชื่อม

bananas -- backed in sweet syrup

luuk chup ลูกชุบ

candy -- beans with jelly glaze

ta' koh ตะโก้

candy -- in palm leaves with coconut creme

khanom bueang ขนมเบื้อง

biscuit, cookie -- with egg yolk and coconut creme or salty with onions

saarim ซาหริ่ม

candy noodles -- with sugar peas, coconut milk and crushed ice

RESTAURANT & BAR

At the restaurant

A table for two, please.
To' samrap sawng khon.
โต๊ะสำหรับสองคน

I am expecting some friends.
Phom kamlang raw phuean.
ผมกำลังรอเพื่อน

Can I see the menu.
Khaw menuu noi khrap.
ขอเมนูหน่อยครับ

I did not order this.
Phom mai dai sang jaan nee.
ผมไม่ได้สั่งจานนี้

Did you order already ?
Sang laeo rue yang khrap ?
สั่งแล้วหรือยังครับ

RESTAURANT & BAR

I did not eat yet.

Phom yang mai dai thaan khaao.
ผมยังไม่ได้ทานข้าว

What would you like to eat ?

Khun yaak thaan arai ?
คุณอยากทานอะไร

Would you like to taste ?

Chim noi mai ?
ชิมหน่อยไหม

That looks delicious.

Duu naa thaan.
ดูน่าทาน

That smells delicious.

Hawm naa thaan.
หอมน่าทาน

Restaurant & Bar

Delicious ?
Aroi mai ?
อร่อยไหม

Very delicious.
Aroi maak.
อร่อยมาก

Are you still hungry ?
Im laeo rue yang ?
อิ่มแล้วหรือยัง

I am full.
Im laeo.
อิ่มแล้ว

Pay, please ! The bill, please !
Kep ngoen duai ! Chek bin duai !
เก็บเงินด้วย/ เช็คบิลด้วย

RESTAURANT & BAR

In the bar

I am thirsty.
Hĭw nám.
หิวน้ำ

What would you like to drink?
Khun tâwng kaan dùem àrai ?
คุณต้องการดื่มอะไร

I want to drink beer.
Yàak dùem bia.
อยากดื่มเบียร์

Cheers!
Chon kâeo !
ชนแก้ว

Restaurant & Bar

You can drink!
Duem keng jang.
ดื่มเก่งจัง

How much did you drink already?
Khun duem kee kaeo laeo?
คุณดื่มกี่แก้วแล้ว

Are you drunk?
Mao laeo rue yang?
เมาแล้วหรือยัง

Didn't you drink a little bit too much?
Mao maak pai rue plao?
เมามากไปหรือเปล่า

You better stop drinking now.
Naa ja' yut duem dai laeo.
น่าจะหยุดดื่มได้แล้ว

RESTAURANT & BAR

INDEX

A

abandon 32
able 25
above 125
abroad 124
academy 87
accident 120
accompany 28
account 101
add 28
address 124
advertise 28
afraid 136
after 63
after tomorrow 60
afternoon 58, 60
ago 63
agree 28
ahead 125
air 113
aircondition 117
airmail 101
airplane 117
airport 117
almost 63
alone 139
already 50
also 50
although 50
always 63
ambitious 136
and 50

and then 50
angry 132, 136
animal 111
ankle 95
announce 28
annoyed 136
answer 28, 50, 107
ant 111
apple 157
appointment 63
approximate 63
April 61
arm 95
around 125
around the world 125
arrival 117
arrive 28
as far as 126
ashtray 154
ask 25
aspirin 99
assemble 31
assist 28
assume 28
at 63, 126
attack 28
attempt 36
August 61
aunt 90
Australia 125

B

back 95

bad 39
bag 72
bake 158
banana 157
bananas 175
bandage 99
bank 101
bathroom 80
bathtub 80
bay 113
be 25
beach 113
beard 95
beautiful 42, 144
because 50
bed 82
bedroom 82
beef 173
beef salad 164
beer 179
before 63
before yesterday 60
begin 28, 36
beginning of month 61
behind 125
believe 28
belt 71
beside 126
bet 28
bicycle 117
big 39, 75
bigger 75

INDEX

biggest 75
bill 107, 178
bird 111
biscuit 175
bite 98
bitter 159
black 74
blanket 82
blood 95
blossom 28
blouse 71
blue 74
body 95
boil 158
boiled eggs 163
bone 95
bookshelf 80
bored 136
borrow 28, 102
bottle 154
bottle opener 81, 154
bottom 95
bowl 154
box 101
brain 95
brave 136
bread 163
break 28, 120
break down 120
breakfast 153
breast 95
breeze 113
brother 89
brown 74
brush 72

build 29
burn 97
bus 117
bus station 117
bus stop 117
businessman 87
busy 108
but 50
butter 163
butterfly 111
buttocks 95
buy 25
bye 22

C

call 29
calm 132, 149
Cambodia 125
can 25
canal 113
cancel 29
candy 175
candy noodles 175
cap 71
cape 113
capital 124
capital city 124
car 117, 120
car park 120
car rental charge 120
careless 131
carpet 79
carry 25
cars 54
case 50
cashew nuts 162

cat 111
celebrate 29
century 62
chair 80, 154
change 29, 102
channel 113
chase 29
cheap 39
cheaper 76
check 29, 103
cheek 95
cheerful 136
Cheers 179
cheque 101
chest 95
chicken 111, 173
chicken on rice 168
chicken salad 164
chicken soup 166
children 54
chilli 161
chilli paste 161
chilli powder 161
chilli sauce 160
chin 95
chips 162
chopped 158
chopsticks 154
cigarettes 154
city 124
clams 170, 171
clean 27, 39
clear 35
clever 41
climb 29
clock 59

183

INDEX

close 29
closet 82
clothes 71
cloud 113
clumsy 41
coast 113
coat hanger 82
cockle 170
cockroach 111
coconut 157
coffee 155
cold 40, 97
collect 29
collect call 107
college 87
colour 74
comb 72
come 25
come for 34
command 29
company 87
complain 29
concentrate 135
concerned 133
confident 134
confused 136
connect 107
considerate 134
constant 63
convince 29
cook 29, 86, 158
cookie 175
cooking pot 81
cool 132, 149
cool season 62
corner 125

correct 29
cotton 72
cough 97
count 29
country 124
courageous 136
cow 111
cowardly 136
crab 170, 172
crash helmet 117
crazy 136
crisp 159
crisp noodles 169
crocodile 111
cry 29, 146
cup 154
cupboard 81
curious 136
curry 167
cut 29
cute 144

D

daily 94
dance 30
dangerous 39
dark 39
dark blue 74
dark brown 74
dark green 74
date 62, 63
daughter 89
daughter-in-law 90
day 60
deal 37
debt 102

December 61
deep 41
deep fry 158
delicious 177
deliver 30
dentist 86, 93
departure 117
deposit 102
detour 120
diarrhoea 97
diet 99
different 76
difficult 39
dig 30
diligent 136
dinner 153
dirty 39
disappointed 136
discover 30
disease 97
district 124
distrustful 136
divide 30
dizzy 93
do 25
doctor 86, 93
document 117
dog 111
done 158
door 79
double bed 118
dozen 54
drawer 82
dream 30
dress 71
drink

25, 139, 154, 179
drive 120
driving licence 121
drunk 180
duck 111
duck salad 164
durian 157
dust 30
dustbin 81

E

ear 95
earn 102
east 124
easy 39
eat 25, 154, 177
economical 102
egg 163
egg noodles 165
egg yolk 174
elbow 95
electrician 86
elephant 112
elevator 79
employee 85
empty 39
end 30
end of month 61
engineer 86
England 125
entrance 79
envelope 101
envious 137
escape 30
Europe 124
evening 58, 60

ever 63
exam 87
examine 29, 99
excited 137
exercise 99
exit 79
expensive 39, 76
explain 30
export 30
express 101
express train 123
eye 95
eyebrow 95

F

face 95
factory 87
faint 98
faintness 94
false 137
family 89
far 40
farmer 86
fast train 123
fat 39
father 89
father-in-law 90
February 61
feed 30
feel 30
fence 79
ferry 117
fever 98
field 113
fill up 120
find 25, 30

fine 20
finger 96
fingernail 96
finish 30
fire 113
first 54
first class 123
fisch sauce 160
fish 112, 170, 171
fish cake 162
fish sauce 159
fish soup 166
fisherman 86
flavour 159
flee 30
flirt 31
flooding 114
floor 79
flower 111
flu 98
fly 112
follow 31
food 153, 154
foot 96
forecast 31
forehead 96
forest 114
forget 25
fork 154
fracture 98
free time 140
Friday 60
fridge 81
fried eggs 163
fried noodles 169
fried rice 173

INDEX

frog 112
front 125
fruit juices 156
fruits 156
frustrated 137
fry 31, 158
frying pan 81
full 39
fun 149
furious 136

G

gain 31
garage 121
garbage bin 81
garden 79
gather 31
generous 132
genitals 96
get up 31
girlfriend 46
give 25, 31
glad 20, 131
glass 154
glass noodle salad 164
gloves 71
go 25
go down 31
go out 25
go up 31
gold 74
good 39
Good Afternoon 19
Good Evening 19
Good Morning 19

grab 36
grandchild 89
grandfather 90
grandmother 90
grape 157
grass 111
green 74
GREETINGS 18
grey 74
grill 158
grow 31
guava 157
guess 36

H

hair 96
hair shampoo 72
hairdresser 86
half 59, 120
half boiled eggs 163
hand 96
hand-made 72
handsome 144
handy 107
hang 31
happen 31
happy 135, 137, 150
harbour 117
hard 40
hat 71
hate 31
have 25
he 19
head 96
health 99

hear 25
heart 96, 131, 133
heartbroken 135
heavy 40
helmet 117
Help 95
help 26, 28
her 19
here 125
hide 31
high tide 114
hip 96
his 19
hit 31
hobby 85
honest 133
honey 163
hoover 37
hope 32
horse 112
hospital 93
hot 40, 159
hot dog 162
hot season 62
hotel 117
hour 59
house 79
How 45
How far 45
How many 45
How much 45
hungry 152, 178
hunt 32
hurt 94, 98, 133
husband 89

INDEX

I

I 19
ice 155
ice cubes 155
ice-skate 32
if 50
ill 98
illegal 40
illness 97
import 32
impressed 135
in 63, 126
in case of 50
in front 125
in the middle of 126
in this moment 63
in time 63
infection 98
influenced 132
influenza 98
injection 99
injury 98
insect bite 98
inside 126
insurance 121
interest 101
interested 135
interrupt 32
intersection 121
invent 32
invite 32
island 113
it 19

J

jacket 71
jackfruit 157
jam 163
January 61
jealous 137
joke 32
journey 128
juices 156
July 61
jump 32
junction 121
June 61
jungle 113
just 63
just now 63

K

kangaroo 112
kick 32
kind 72, 134
kiss 32
kitchen 81
kitchen cupboard 81
knee 96
knife 154
knock 32
know 26

L

ladder 79
lake 113
lamp 82
lane 124
Laos 125
last 54, 63
late 63
later 22
laugh 26
launder 27
lawyer 86
lazy 137
lease 33, 35
leather 72
leave 32
left 125
left-luggage office 123
leg 96
legal 40
lend 33, 102
let 33
letter 101
letterbox 101
library 79
lie 33
lift 34, 79
light 39, 40
light blue 74
light green 74
lighter 154
like 26
lime 157
line 108
lion 112
lip 96
lipstick 72
listen 33

187

little 40
live 26, 48, 140
liver 96
living room 81
lizard 112
lobster 170, 172
lonely 137
long 41, 77
longan 157
look 26
look after 33
look for 26
lose 33
lot 40
loud 40
love 26, 137
love triangle 137
lovesickness 137
low tide 114
luck 22
luggage 119
lunch 153
lung 96
lychee 157

M

made 72
maid 86
mailbox 101
make 25
make - up 72
make-up table 82
Malaysia 125
manage 33
manager 87
mango 157
mangosteen 157
March 61
market 47, 72, 154
marmalade 163
marry 33
matches 154
mattress 82
May 61
maybe 50
mean 137
meat balls 162
mechanic 86
medical treatment 99
medicine 99
meeting 63
menu 154, 176
message 109
microwave 81
middle 126
milk 155
mine 19
minute 59
mirror 80
miss 137
misunderstand 33
mixed salad 164
mobile phone 107
Monday 60
money 101, 102
monkey 112
month 61
mood 136
moody 136
moon 113
morning 57, 60
mosquito 112
mother 89
mother-in-law 90
motorbike 117
mountain 113
mouse 112
mouth 96
mow 33
multiply 33
muscle 96
musician 86
mussels 170, 172
must 26
mustache 96
my 19
Myanmar 125

N

nail scissors 72
name 20, 139
napkin 155
narrow 42
near 40
nearly 63
neat 41
neck 96
need 26, 33
nephew 90
nerve 96
nervous 137
nevertheless 50
new 40
next 64
next to 126
nice 131
nicknames 150
niece 90

INDEX

night 56, 60
night snack 153
no 49
Nobody 108
noodle soup 165
noodles 165, 169
normally 64
north 124
nose 97
not yet 50
November 61
nurse 86, 93
nuts 162

O

October 61
offer 72
often 140
okay 151
old 40
omelet 163
on 63
on time 64
only 50
open 33
opener 81, 154
operator 107
opposite 126
or 50
or not yet 50
orange 74, 157
orchid 111
order 33, 176
ordinary 41
our 19
outside 126

oven 81
over there 126
overseas 107
overseas call 107
owner 87
oyster 170, 172
oyster sauce 161

P

pain 98
painkiller 99
paint 34
painter 86
pair 54
palm tree 111
pan 81
papaya 157
papaya salad 162
parcel 101
parents 89
park 121
parrot 112
passport 103
pay 26, 34
peanuts 162
pepper 159
perch 170
perfume 72
perhaps 50
permanent 63
persuade 34
petrol station 121
phone 29, 107
photographer 86
pick up 34
pig 112

pill 99
pillow 82
pilot 86
pineapple 157
pineapple juice 156
pink 74
pity 137
plaster 99
plate 155
platform 123
play 26
playful 137
pleasant 131
pleased 133
plenty 40
plough 34
plow 34
point to 34
policeman 86
pomelo 157
pool 79
poor 41
pork 173
pork on rice 168
pork salad 164
porridge 165
possibly 50
post card 101
post office 101
postman 86
pot 81
potato chips 162
pour 34
powder 72
prawn 170
prawn salad 164

prawn soup 166
prawns 172, 173
precinct 124
predict 31
prescription 99
present 72
prevent 34
previous 63
primary school 87
produce 34
profession 85
pronounce 22
proud 134
province 124
pudding 174
pull 34
punch 34
punish 34
pupil 87
push 34
put on 71
pyjamas 71

Q

quality 72
quarrel 34
question 44, 50
quick 41
quiet 40

R

rabbit 112
radio 80
railway 117, 123
railway station 117, 123
rainy season 62
rambutan 158
rat 112
raw 158
razor 72
read 26
ready 151
receipt 101
receive 35, 102
red 74
reduce 76
refuel 121
regards 22
register 35, 102
regret 135
relatives 90
remember 26
remove 35
renew 35
rent 33, 35, 78
repair 35, 122
require 33
reservation 123
reside 26
respect 35
rest 35
restaurant 153
return ticket 123
rice 169
rice and pork 168
rice porridge 165
rice soup 165
rich 41
ride 36
right 42, 125

ring 32
ripe 41
river 114
river crab 170
roasted eggs 162
roseapple 158
run 35
ruthless 131

S

sad 135
safe 39, 119
salad 164
sale 72
salt 159
salty 159
sand 114
sandal 71
satay 162
Saturday 60
sauce 159
sausage salad 164
save 102
school 87
scrambled eggs 163
sea 114
seafood 170
seafood curry 167
seafood salad 164
seafood soup 166
seaport 117
search 26
season 62
second 59
secondary school 87
secretary 87

INDEX

see 26
sell 26
send 35, 102
sensitive 132
September 61
service 155
sew 36
shallow 41
shampoo 27, 72
shark 170
shave 73
shaver 72
shaving cream 72
she 19
ship 117
shirt 71
shoe 71
shoot 35
shop 87
shopping 75
short 41, 77
short cut 121
shoulder 97
shout 35
shrimp chips 162
shrimp paste 160
shrimp sauce 160
shrimps 172
shy 137
siblings 47, 89
sick 93, 98
silk 72
silly 41
silver 74
since 64
sing 35

sink 81
sister 89
sit 26
size 77
skilful 41
skin 97
skirt 71
sky 114
sleep 26
sleeping car 123
sleeping pill 99
slim 39
slimming 35
slow 41
small 39
smell 35
smile 26, 144
smoke 35
smoking 155
snack 162
snake 112
soap 72
sock 71
sofa 80
soft 40
soldier 87
sole 97
sometimes 64
son 89
son-in-law 90
soon 22, 64
sore throat 98
sorrow 135
Sorry 64
sort 72
sour 159

south 124
soy sauce 161
spare ribs 162
speak 27, 46
special 41, 72
spell 35
spend 102
spicy 159
spider 112
spoon 155
sprain 98
spring roll 162
squid 170, 171
squid salad 164
stairs 79
stamp 101
stand 36
star 114
start 28, 36
steam 158
steer 120
stew 158
sticky rice 169, 174
still 63
stingy 137
stitch 36
stomach 97
stone 114
stop 121
storey 79
stove 81
straight ahead 125
street 124
strong 42
student 87
subtract 36

191

sugar 159
sugarapple 158
suggest 36
suit 72
sun 114
sunburn 98
Sunday 60
sunglasses 47
sunrise 114
sunset 114
suppose 36
sure 134
surprised 134
sweat 97
sweater 72
sweet 155, 159
sweet & sour 159
sweets 174
swim 27
swimming pool 79

T

T-shirt 72
table 80, 155
tablecloth 155
tablet 99
tailor 72, 87
take 27
take a ride 121
take care 33
take off 71
take over 121
tamarind 158
taste 36, 159, 177
tasteless 159
tea 156
teach 36
teacher 87
tears 146
telegram 101
telephone 80, 107
telephone bill 107
telephone book 107
telephone box 107
telephone number 107
television 80
tell 27
test 87
Thailand 124
theirs 19
there 126
thermos flask 81
they 19
thick 39
thin 39
think 36
thirsty 152, 179
throw 36
Thursday 60
ticket 123
ticket office 123
tide 114
tidy 41
tiger 112
tiger prawn 170
tight 77
time 54, 56, 59
timetable 123
toast 158
today 60
toenail 97
toilet 80
tomorrow 22, 60
tones 10
tongue 97
too 50
tooth 97
toothbrush 72
toothpaste 72
toothpick 155
touch 36
tow off 121
towel 72
town 124
traffic 121
traffic jam 121, 127
traffic lights 121
train 123
translate 36
travel 36
traveller's cheque 101
tree 111
trouser 72
try 36, 42, 77
Tuesday 60
tuna 170
turn 121
turn around 121
turtle 112
twin beds 118
type 72, 102
tyre pressure 122

U

ugly 42
uncle 90

INDEX

unconscious 98
under 126
understand 27, 133
university 87
unripe 41
untidy 41
up to 126
upset 132
urgent 64
USA 125

V

vaccuum 37
vegetable 173
vegetable soup 166
village 124
vinegar 159, 160
violet 74
visit 37
vomit 98

W

waist 97
wait 27
waiter 155
wake up 37
walk 31, 37
wall 79
want 26, 27
wardrobe 82
wash 27
washbasin 80
waste 37, 102
waste of time 64
watch 59

water 155
water tap 80
waterfall 114
watermelon 158
we 19
weak 42, 94
weather 114
Wednesday 60
week 61
weekend 61
Welcome 20
west 124
wet 42
What 45
When 45
when 50, 63
Whenever 67
Where 45
Where from 45
Where to 45
Which 45
Which way 45
whisper 37
white 74
Who 45
Why 45
wide 42, 77
wife 89
win 37
wind 113
window 79
windy 113
wipe 37
with 50
withdraw 102
wonderful 144

wonton 165
wood 114
work 27, 46
work on 37
worker 85
world 124
worried 133, 137
wound 98
wrist 97
write 27
wrong 42, 108

Y

year 62
yellow 74
yes 49
yesterday 60
yet 50
you 19
young 40
yours 19

Z

zoo 111

193

www.bangkokbooks.com

Need to know more ?
The fun way to learn the language !

E_{NGLISH} - T_{HAI}

The fun way to learn the language...

Includes colloquial Thai !

www.bangkokbooks.com